Ancient Voices
Ever Singing

Poems of Britain's
spiritual history

Tony Leonard

Loistavat
Books

11 Nightingale Crescent
Leatherhead
KT24 6PD
United Kingdom

First edition published in the United Kingdom by Loistavat Books (2016).

ISBN: 978-1-911086-22-2
Cover design: LM Graphic Design

About the Author

Tony Leonard was born in the fenland town of Soham, nestled between the borders of Suffolk and Norfolk in Cambridgeshire. He enjoyed the outdoor life in the countryside as a boy, building up his collection of birds' eggs, absorbing the beautiful atmosphere. He was a dreamer, mischievous and lively by nature, also highly impressionable and sensitive, however his upper class music teacher had a good influence on him, introducing him to poetry, playing the piano and singing; much to her delight, he appeared on stage winning prizes as a boy soprano.

Slight in build, Tony was not suited for farm work, even though his father was a pig farmer and market gardener, so he spent his youth training as a piano tuner. When he became fully qualified he met many interesting people and places, from the universities in Cambridge to stately homes and idyllic thatched cottages in Essex.

During this time, he was surrounded by a wealth of knowledge and he became interested in medieval history, folklore and mythology; unfortunately, this led to a fascination for the supernatural, magic and the occult. He foolishly sought power and thought this would compensate for his lack of academic achievements. The climax came one evening in a village just outside Cambridge, where he met some academic artists who attempted to get him to join them on the astral plain, as he'd experienced a pagan rebirth. Somehow he realised his soul was in peril in this weird setup; the decadent paintings and the totem poles situated in the garden. Tony was filled with terror and remorse, and he sought a safe haven.

Now in his retirement years he lives with his understanding and supportive wife Joy and he's appreciative of her grandsons, Daniel and Luke, for their computer skills. Tony plays the piano in the mornings and has an extensive romantic and classical repertoire. The afternoons are then spent writing plays or poetry, and he often does recitations in his local town of Saint Ives.

Endorsements

Tony Leonard's passion for poetry is second to none, his words ring through with the clarity and stark reality of the ages, their integrity is derived from the deep research that he conducts on all the varied subjects of his poetry.

Christopher Morgan
Published Poet and Mayors Poet of St Ives Cambs 2015/16
Regular host of St Ives Poetry Folk bi-monthly gatherings

Tony Leonard's poetry tends to creep up on you and hit you hard. For example, in his work 'Saint Ivo in Slepe' I feel he takes us on a dark journey into a sinister world of what is effectively prehistory. This is skilful as it is as if he has somehow captured a video of all those years ago. Reading it I felt both cold and frightened; shocked at what I was seeing in my mind's eye.

In the poem 'The Prize' there are again strong images but there is a lightness that almost leads me to disregard the brutal acts of the era. It also moves with the rapidity of a modern fantasy movie leaving the reader thoroughly entertained but breathless.

I do not see myself as a poet but more as a lyricist. In that genre you have to convey the emotion from the very start. What I really like about Tony's work is that he pulls you in from the beginning and holds you there for what are often quite long journeys. He paints vivid pictures but in sketch form, leaving you, the reader, to fill in the image details from who you are and how you see the world. This is the art of high aesthetics. The more you learn about yourself the more you appreciate the piece. There is therefore much to appreciate in Tony's work.

Chris Lewis
Professor
Aver Psychology, PE 27 5 JB

Contents

Preface

T. S. Elliot wrote, 'Time present and time past are perhaps present in time future.' These collective poems seek to take you on a journey back into the past in order to clarify the future and provide you with a spiritual map and compass to understand the present.

We all enjoy the comforts that most of us have in today's world with its unprecedented and sophisticated science and technology, as well as its celebrity culture. Some would have us believe we've evolved or developed and are superior to any previous age. In many respects this may be true, at least in a temporal sense; so can we rest on our laurels and enjoy the euphoria, or have we been brainwashed?

In the bee kingdom, a drone feeds on the golden honeycomb, mates with the queen (if he's lucky) but dies for the privilege; the surviving drones are stung to death if they attempt to escape from this tyranny. The worker bee, however, soars merrily in the spirit from flower to flower in the summer sun in freedom. The burning question is, have we become like the drones and come under a yoke of slavery, from which our ancestors were set free and built a rich spiritual heritage that made this country great?

It's time for us to move on in our journey back into the dark medieval period, with no distractions from modern technology. First we will make a brief visit to the misty and haunting fens. Then we will move on to the Anglo Saxon and Celtic saints, meeting with their adversaries, religion, magic and politics, expressed through their shrines, rivers, streams, bubbling springs and groves, and experience their passionate soul power in nature.

Next we will move back and see how ancient Druidism is alive and well in present day society, and also how the biblical Babylon has influenced architecture in urban culture. As you'll find, everything is not quite what it seems.

Finally, we will meet some brave folk who've already made this journey through the past centuries, engaging with these timeless forces rearing their ugly heads today, with some under a different guise. The reward for the overcomers is the ability to see through the liberal fog and not perceive white as black and black as white; their true national identity will be restored.

Country Characters and Craftsmen

The collection begins with 'A Ghostly Village'. A seasoned traveller feels the village is lifeless and caught in the grip of death; he observes how the current generation have turned their backs on its traditions and are oblivious to the pervading dark forces.

The traveller decides to go back in time a hundred years to see the village brought to life again through its characters and craftsmen, but finds that superstition and magic still play their part.

A Ghostly Village

A seasoned traveller wandered through the shire,
Passed by many milestones on country roads,
How he loved to tread those pilgrims' paths,
By gipsy caravans down haunted droves.

During his travels he came to an old gnarled oak,
Its thick rounded trunk reached a staggering height,
Its bleached white branches, twisted crooked hands,
All covered with scores of crows, as black as night.

Beneath the summer sun's scorching rays,
He sniffed those yellow fields, so parched and stale,
Shimmering there in a trembling heat haze,
And timbered buildings nestled in the vale.

He felt a witch's presence pierce through time
And he quickly crossed the hump stone bridge,
Overheard her whispering her eerie rhyme,
There on his way into this ghostly village.

When he opened the churchyard's creaking gate,
Saw how the moss had mottled every grave,
How they leaned there in a drunken state,
Where he felt their departed spirits rave.

He's saddened ivy clings and covers the church,
And once inside he's touched by dangling cobwebs.
He stood before a sacred Saxon font,
Portrayed an innocence now killed stone dead.

He watched a sexton's spirit sounding the bell,
Stared at him from all those years ago,
He faced some demons, torturing the damned in flames,
Seen there glowing on a stained glass window.

Down by a shady river, he came to a wood
That led to a path close by a castle mound.
He came to priory ruins, heard phantom monks
Chant in Latin on this holy ground.

Underneath a thatched country cottage,
He listened a while to rap and heavy rock,
This music lifted his spirit but wound him up,
Now he's driven by the Devil's clock.

That thought of innocent children on computers
Up in their bedrooms, behind closed doors,
Playing games with demons which haunted hermits,
Come from where the Prince of Darkness soars.

All round the vale he felt the evil forces
That drained his spirit like a dried up well,
He saw dark angels mounted on their horses,
Surround the sleepy village, entombed in this hell.

He dragged himself up to the top of Hangman's Hill,
And found this sense of darkness zapped his zeal,
So shocked to see that derelict watermill,
With piles of weeds wrapped round its broken wheel.

An old farmyard soon filled his heart with strife,
That rusty plough and weeds in rotting wain,
He wondered whatever had happened to village life
And found it set his eternal spark aflame.

Gipsy Girl

One day a red-haired gipsy girl
Skipped along in her usual flare,
Going round from door to door,
Through the Suffolk town of Clare,
After she'd read the people's palms,
Sold her pegs and yards of lace,
Sometimes she gave them lucky charms,
With that smiling, fresh country face.

The beauty of her heaving breast
Seemed to heighten her summery glow,
Swishing around in a scarlet skirt,
Through flowery meadows on tiptoe,
Such sweet songs came from her lips,
On the priory's sacred ground,
Passed a river, swaying her hips,
There by a castle's wooded mound.

Often she'd walk in late evening,
Under those skies of red and mauve,
Smelt the simmering stew in a cauldron,
On that fire in a darkening drove.
When she went to do her chores,
Enchanted by a nightingale,
Dark moths fluttered round her lamp,
Silver moonbeams lit up the vale.

She clicked her fingers to gipsy guitars,
Spellbound by the crackling fire,
Under that dome of sparkling stars,
Found it touched her deepest desire.
She danced well into the night,
Moved so wildly to the beat,
Inside the clapping gipsies' circle,
Around her camp with bare white feet.

At dawn, she arose so full of zeal,
Guided her horses' leather reins,
Adored the sound of caravan wheels
And horses clopping down the lanes,
Thundering over a hump stone bridge,
Her Romany spirit so full of glee,
Journeyed on through town and village,
With her heart so wild and free.

Blacksmith's Dream

One evening my ears pricked up as I left the George
And Dragon, when the old church clock struck nine,
I ran down Friday Lane to my fiery forge;

My hammer rang on my anvil in rhythm and rhyme,
Beads of sweat dripped down my beaten brow,
Would I get those horseshoes done in time?

I saw those red horned imps, who fared so foul,
In those burning coals, that fired up my dream,
Had roused the spark inside my pent-up soul,

That night a brewing tempest disturbed the stream,
I saw forked lightning split an oak asunder,
Then burst in flames and lit up the village green.

A pervading presence filled my spirit with wonder,
Those horrifying hounds and hunter's horn
And the galloping horses in the thunder.

How I revelled in this raging storm,
The sound of hooves clopping down the street,
At a time that overshadowed the dawn.

There I stood almost dead on my feet,
Faced that Saxon god in his broad brimmed hat,
The two crows on his shoulders looked so bleak.

I turned, saw Sleipnir's hide, glistening in black;
I froze with fear and thought my end was nigh,
But nailed his eight horseshoes on all intact,

Under Woden's giant red glowing eye,
Then I watched him ride back into the sky.

Milkmaid

This young, glorious golden-haired milkmaid
Rose in the dawn and looked so live and alert,
Like those bubbling springs in Greenwood Glade,

She sang and danced along her way to work,
Her heaving bosom hugged her low cut blouse,
Swished around in a long, red gipsy skirt,

Adored the blossom hanging from the boughs,
That leafy copse and bluebells out in bloom,
The cuckoo and nightingale that seemed to arouse

Her thoughts about the stars and crescent moon,
There with her lover in a flowery bed,
Under that spell from the owlet's haunting tune,

As she squeezed the cow's teats in the shed
And squirted its milk into a wooden bucket,
Counting off the days when she'll be wed,

Dreamed about last summer when they first met,
The time was ripe to shed her heavy yoke;
She moved forward with hope at every step,

And told the giggly girls about her bloke,
Welcomed the coolness in the local dairy,
Could barely wait for evening, when she'll elope.

Later she found herself in Buttercup Lea,
Stood awhile and watched the trilling high lark,
She felt her soaring spirit was just as free
From the love that welled up in her heart.

The Butcher

Clive, a local butcher,
Nicknamed the laughing clown,
Down at the summer fair,
With people gathered round.

Sometimes he was sad
And very highly strung,
Though liked to be seen
There having a bit of fun.

Those rockets tied to his back
He itched to light the fuse,
Thought this the only cure,
End his fit from the blues.

Often he played the fool,
Went in the air with a whiz!
He let out such a shout,
Now he'd run out of fizz.

All up high in the sky,
Found he'd gone amiss,
In a pond with a splash,
That emptied it of fish.

The Baker

Sorrow struck the baker's house;
He closed his curtains that dark day,
Sat there mourning, quiet as a mouse,
Now his wife had passed away.

He watched her on the bed at rest,
Sat and wrote to her next of kin,
Laid a pile of breadcrumbs on her chest,
And hoped it would draw out her sin.

Down the stone steps in his bakery,
He kneaded large batches of dough,
Pitted, patted and got it right,
Put them in his oven just so.

When he stoked his oven fire,
Those burning coals made such a roar,
Red imps spat at him in fury,
Then all jumped out on the floor.

Later he looked inside his oven,
Shocked on seeing the shapes of bread,
Baked there flat, all six in a row,
Just like bodies, lying dead.

All night he feared he'd come to harm,
His thoughts went back to Ethel Green,
The witch, who gave his wife a charm,
There on her way to Halloween.

He heard the church's funeral bell,
Took those pennies off her eyes,
Surprised to see them blaze like hell
And her body began to rise.

The Candlestick Maker

Darkness gripped him in the swirling fog,
After the backbreaking toil
On a pagan site, he dug up a log,
All blackened by the fenland soil.

He worked like a man possessed by his craft
Carving out his candlestick,
Spurred on by some visions from the past
And felt empathy with its spirit.

Seized by a sense of ritual, he lit his candle
And stared into its naked flame.
It lit his fire, which burned within his breast,
Felt that ancient feast of Beltane.

A branch of green leaves spread all around,
A blood stained altar under an oak,
He saw a Druid lurking in the shadows,
His skull smiled from his hooded cloak.

He faced this high priest holding a budding crook
That sent him into a strange trance,
When those forces of nature entered his body,
Found an inner urge to dance.

Now he'd been drawn in that other world,
Formed a bond with the Celtic dead,
He glanced in his mirror, saw how much he'd aged,
Heaviness weighed on his soul like lead.

After a while, he snuffed his candle out,
To relieve the torment in his mind,
He shook there in his room, totally pitch black,
Not able to break from eternal time.

Steeplejack

A steeplejack climbed his lofty ladder,
To clean the weathervane and grey church spire,
His ears pricked up to the stirring organ,
Angelic voices from a heavenly choir.
He loved this music that soared through the air
And looked down on the garland wishing well,
Amidst that bustling at the springtime fair,
Where maidens swished around on a carousel,
May blossom decked those doors along the street,
Those Morris dancers on the village green,
Their frenzied feet in time with piper's beat,
Children splashing in a bubbling stream,
He adored this bird's eye view of village life,
Here in merry England all free from strife.

Haymaker's Passion

Young Jack pitches the hay,
Maiden passes his way,
Sees that glint in her eyes,
Takes him by surprise,
There one summer's day.

Licks his lusty lips,
Watches her swaying hips,
Loves the way she's dressed,
With her heaving breast,
Seem so hard to resist.

Oh, that long dark hair,
Features fine and fair,
Sitting down in his cart,
Messes with his heart,
That he longs to share.

'Come this summer's day,
Lie on my bed of hay,'
But she breaks his embrace,
Slaps him round his face,
Sad, she runs away.

Gravedigger

Winston dug six feet with his spade;
He struck a pile of brittle bones,
Unaware he'd found a Saxon grave,
Where he heard some moans and groans.
He felt he'd pierced the realms of time,
Bent down, picked up a silver crown,
Couldn't believe he'd made such a find,
Amazed how its glory shone around,
He stood before a king and queen,
That made his spirit rise in his heart.
Now its saints were seen on the green,
Found it rekindled his Christian spark.
He saw Saint Edmund's ghost in a field
Display three silver crowns on his shield.

Father Brown

Father Brown went through his rectory gate,
That led beneath his avenue of chestnut trees,
He watched those rooks wheeling their sign of fate,
Above the autumn falling golden leaves.
He wore a black cape and looked like a figure of death,
His strict movements came from his disciplined will,
He muttered his thoughts, from his steaming breath,
In his parish, that seemed so lifeless and still.

Often he walked aloof around his village,
This well-built man, overbearing in height,
Cultured and spent so many hours in study,
He always finished before the stroke of midnight,
Since that dark night when the howling storm
Drove the winter wind and pouring rain,
He saw his former rector's ghostly face
Stare at him right through his window pane.

How he loved and treasured his Oxford oar
And graduation portrait that hung in his hall,
He took great pride in his intellectual power
With his many fine books that lined his wall.
He studied passages from God's Holy Word,
But his religious rites had led him into sin,
It seemed he preferred the scholarship from men,
That fired his idolatry that burned within.

One Sunday he began a requiem mass for the dead
Haunted by chiming from the old church clock,
He thought about that ghostly rector, who'd led
Departed souls astray and let down his flock.
How he sweated and fingered beads on his rosary,
Wondering why he'd followed church tradition,
He crossed himself and fell upon his knees,
Found this road that led to superstition.

Sometimes he thought about heaven and hell,
There in the organ music's gentle flow,
He joined his church choir, singing a Bach chorale,
Lifted his gaze to a stained glass window,
Golden shafts of light streamed down from the Lamb.
He found another image entered his mind,
The grinning face of disgorging Green Man,
That haunted his soul down through those years in time.

He spoke the liturgy in Latin from his lips,
There in the sanctuary on holy ground,
He rang a bell among incense and music,
Served the mass to those all gathered round.
When the organ's music shook the floor,
He felt his hair stand up on the back of his hand,
The spirit of Antichrist that made him glow
With the bane that overshadowed England.

He saw that ghostly rector in rising incense
Lurk there inside the Lady Chapel,
This image burned so brightly in his mind,
That courted the spirit of death that came from hell.
He watched him rise to the Gothic roof in height,
Enshrouded in evil from ancient Babylon,
Father Brown's long face had turned so white,
Now his soul's dragged down to the dragon's den.

Ethel Green

Ethel Green, a local witch,
Couldn't believe her luck,
When given two evil spirits,
Named them Quince and Puck.
She clicked her heels and laughed in glee,
Showed off her golden tooth,
At night she saw a demon stare,
When lifting up her roof.

There she stood in her steaming kitchen,
Her cauldron hung on chains,
She stirred the bubbling brew inside,
Its bottom glowed in flames.
She stuck some pins in a waxen doll,
The climax on Halloween,
Her cat meowed, the thunder rolled;
It made her neighbour scream.

She flew out of her bedroom window,
Under a crescent moon,
She whizzed into the heavens,
Astride her crooked broom,
When she reached that astral plain
And heard the demons roar,
Now exalted above those stars,
Her wicked soul did soar.

Well into the night she danced
Around a blazing fire,
With witches between those mossy graves
And ghouls that looked so dire.
She met the princes and powers of the air,
The climax on Halloween,
And right before those bonfire flames,
The Devil crowned her Queen.

The Sorcerer

Thudding of thunder, flashes of light,
Meteors move in those heavens at night,
Flocks of birds that are flying by day,
Wheeling in patterns and show me the way.
Demons of evil now dwell in the air,
Often I'm seen in their awesome flare.
Now when the village is fast asleep,
Then I go down to my castle keep,
Signs of the zodiac's circle on floor,
Lit by black candles and fiend at the door;
See how his magic enhances my craft,
Sparks that spray from my wizard's staff,
I climb up the steps to my castle's old tower,
Summon and ride on those winds of power.
There on the astral high plain I zoom
Passing a round blood red haunting moon,
Here in first heaven among those bright stars,
I, the great sorcerer, strangest of bards,
Feeling this harmony within my soul,
Staring into this giant golden bowl,
Where new stars spring from its wide womb,
Others are dying inside their dark tomb.

Second heaven soon robs me of mirth,
Drifting high over the rounded earth,
Gazing straight down into hell's open jaws,
Shaken by screams and its rumblings and roars,
Choked by the stench from its brimstone breath,
Belly's on fire with the rivers of death,
Watching the demons among those flames,
Scourging the damned in their rattling chains,

I meet the grim reaper now whetting his scythe,
Cringe at the Devil all puffed up in pride,
In hell with its black, bulging heartbeat,
Seeing its kingdom now glowing with heat;
Luminous ley lines link villages, towns,
Pagan sites and those burial mounds.
Now the past blazes before my eyes,
Mithraic temple's grey spirits all rise,
Bearded red sun glowing so bright,
Roman Britain here on this dark night,
With its bubbling clear springs and old wells,
Druids appear in the darkening dells,
Chanting low voices enliven the scene,
Summon their Celtic god Jack in the Green.
When I gaze at the castle on Mars,
How its haunting dark presence jars,
Hearing the creaking from rising portcullis,
Demonic horsemen ride out in the mist,
Princes of power with their leathery wings,
Swarming like bats, the foulest of things,
Magnitude touches my spirit in awe,
Angels and demons with weapons of war,
Clashing and flashing in flames of fire,
Fight for revival of Roman Empire.
Now I can feel all the heavens vibrate,
Seeing the gaping wide jaws of an earthquake,
Deafening roar from its fiery furnace,
Arabian horsemen ride out the abyss.

Light comes streaming straight down from third heaven,
Filling my heart with this following vision,
Shrubs in full blossom and branches of trees,
Bearing incense in this gentle breeze,
Sparkling light gold is embroidered in greenery,
Silvery streams that are dancing so merrily;
Murmur in melody, onward it flows
And it brightens the flowery meadows,
Music enhances their radiant blooms,
Everywhere filled with such beautiful tunes,
Echoes through hills and those lofty vales,
Stirs the enchanting bright nightingales,
Horses now gallop to solo French horn,
Shepherdess watches eternal bright dawn,
Moving around on the hallowed ground,
She's so wrapped up in symphony of sound,
Touching her heart, her wellspring of life,
Fingering notes on her pastoral pipe,
Watching her lambs in their shinning fleece,
See how she's brimming with joy and peace.

There on the top of most sacred of mountains,
Standing between the tall trees and fountains,
Here in the city of New Jerusalem,
Sparkling in numerous kinds of gem;
Streets and its pavements gleaming in gold,
What a glorious sight to behold,
River of crystal that mirrors so clear,
Flowing and heightens the garden's grandeur,
Seasonal fruits so fresh and they shine,
Nourish and flourish where care is divine.

Splendour and beauty in every white mansion,
Everywhere shining as bright as the sun;
Emitting its golden spokes of a wheel,
City vibrates with love and great zeal.

Angelic golden bright trumpets blast,
Here in this kingdom where treasures will last,
Choruses sung by celestial choir,
Seven spirits are breathing their fire;
Here in the heights where this holiness rings,
Giving the glory to King of Kings,
Echoing voices with the Lord of Lords,
Cherubim gripping their glowing swords,
Over the roaring white waterfalls,
Here where the praises and worship enthrals,
Burning bright seraphs around a rainbow,
Dazzled by the Almighty's glow,
Flashing around in the peals of thunder,
Filling the heavens with awe and wonder,
Jesus the lamb has become the lion,
Listen and hear how He roars from Zion.
Shaking the twenty-four judgment thrones,
Watching the four end-time horsemen roam,
This all approved by the Ancient of Days,
There in His glory here all ablaze.

See how my spirit and soul now grieve,
Realise that magic and sorcery deceive,
After many long years of endeavour,
Now I'll be thrown in hell for ever.

Moonraker

A moonraker skipped his feet,
So lively down his village street,
He stared at that moon, shining so bright
And wanted it in his hands that night,
Admired the way it shone in his pond,
He ignored that Devil lurking beyond.
When he started to draw his rake,
That shimmering thing would seem to break.
He looked in those heavens everywhere
And sunk into the depths of despair,
Then down at his feet he saw it all,
When it shone, like a silver ball.
He bounced it, bounced it along the road,
Marvelled how its surface glowed.
After a while he lost control,
Cursed it when it started to roll,
Bent on keeping up the chase,
Annoyed it kept on gathering pace.
He ran out of wind at Fox and Hounds,
Hoped it soon had done its rounds,
He couldn't stop it rolling about,
And saw some drunkards all flake out.
He stopped a moment and laughed with glee,
When an owl fell out of a tree,
The cow jumped over the moon,
That shook a ghost beside his tomb.
He saw it come to a standstill,
There on the brow of Hangman's Hill,
He could hardly believe his eyes
When it leapt back in the starry skies,
Now he'd got rid of this lunatic;
Found his heart cut right to the quick.

The Highwayman

A highwayman sat waiting at Black Horse Drove,
One summer cloudy, moonlit night,
He wore a mask, three cornered hat and cape,
There ready for his chance to strike.

He heard a cracking whip and galloping horses
And sound of the coach's rumbling wheels,
He cocked his musket, aimed and fired his shot,
That made that wounded coachman reel.

He chased the runaway coach for miles on end,
Cursed the clouds of rising dust,
His heart kept pounding, when pursuing his prize;
Found he was driven along by lust.

At last the shiny black coach came to a halt,
He saw Earl Grey's crest on its door,
Countess stepped off the coach, wearing a mask,
Emerald necklace and diamond broach.

The highwayman was captured by her charms,
All dressed for the Earl's masked ball,
He envied those noblemen who'd dance with her,
Who'd remove their masks at the mansion's hall.

He forced the countess to place her jewels in his bag,
Unaware a count came up behind,
Until his swagger stick had cracked his skull,
That finished the highwayman, for all time.

Later the highwayman was brought to trial
And sentenced to death and hung on a gibbet,
But often on a summer moonlit night,
Many have seen his wandering spirit.

The May Queen

How Mary loved the month of May,
Buttercup meadows brightened her way,
That shone on this girl, so fresh and fair,
Who swished her tresses of golden hair,
A lacy white blouse clasped her breast,
In long green skirt so neatly dressed.
She loved the bright red blossoms' hue,
And she looked in those skies so blue.
She heard the chiming church bell,
When she passed Saint Wilfred's well.
Down the road she crossed a bridge;
There on her way into the village,
She crossed the stepping stones in a stream,
That led straight to the village green.

There she danced around a maypole;
A cool light breeze lightened her soul,
Welling up like a bubbling spring,
Bringing nature's every blessing.
She entered into her pagan past,
That she held within her grasp,
She danced around in bare white feet,
In time with Mother Earth's heartbeat,
She took off on those wings of mirth,
Felt at one with spring's rebirth.

A garland of flowers crowned her Queen,
She had a most disturbing dream,
And she looked on an ancient sun;
Her young heart beating like a drum,
She drifted into her pagan past,
Saw her ancestors wearing masks.

These spirits danced with frenzied feet,
She heard their Celtic voices speak,
Lure her into a dance of death,
She shook, with ecstasy on her breath,
Feeling the depth of nature's desires,
There near that blaze from Beltane fires.
She felt the energy of Mother Earth;
Bore its tension of springtime birth,
From all the strain of this dance she died,
Welcomed their spirit as her guide,
And then she felt her spirit hurled
There in the Celtic otherworld.

Passionate Harvest

He loved his ginger-haired, young gipsy girl,
Watched her down on her hands and knees,
Gathering up those severed stalks of wheat,
And she bound them into golden sheaves.
He felt his lover's dark brown roving eyes,
That moved with sweeping sound of his scythe.
He stopped to wipe the sweat upon his brow,
Saw her bright red hair fall on her bosom,
His passion for her cut through the summer air,
Shimmering like heat over those wheat fields,
Like the poppies that fix their scarlet gaze.

Changeling

Autumn came to a woodland glade;
Dark voices whispered in the shade,
How those voices pierced the air,
That came from a bustling elfin fair.
Toadstools' caps were glowing red,
White spots painted on each head,
Fairies and elves danced around,
Their music hardly made a sound.
Sun shone through an evergreen,
Upon an elfin King and Queen:
He wore a beard, so fat and merry,
Her blushing cheeks, red as a cherry,
He sipped his tankard of frothy mead,
And she was piping a hollow reed,
To celebrate their new child's birth,
There in the kingdom of lower earth.
Dusk gave way to shades of night,
That thrilled the heart of every sprite;
They all ran through moonlit meadows,
Came to where a streamlet flows.
They crept around a farmer's house;
There on tiptoe, as quiet as a mouse,
Opened a door where a baby slept.
Into his room those fairies leapt,
Jumped around, their eyes went wild,
They swapped him with their elfin child.
How they laughed and played in a glade,
Being so proud of their evil trade,
They swung in trees from twig to twig;
All finished dancing a lively jig,
There on the grass to an elfin tune,
Under the silver mellow moon.

A Suffolk Ploughman

My Suffolk punches pull my plough
Under the deep red autumn sun,
The rooks, crows and seagulls flock,
Follow where my furrows run.

Beneath the pink and purple skies,
I guide my plough, enjoy that feel,
My horses' hooves thud on the earth,
And hear my plough's squeaky wheel.

A seasoned silver moon that shines
Over the furrows of my field;
I gaze in this kingdom of golden stars,
That grants an everlasting shield.

My spirit rises up like a fountain
And stars begin to speak their joys,
Sparkling deep within my breast;
There in my seat of harmonic poise.

I move around in those musical spheres
And hear an inspiring angelic choir;
This heavenly music moves me to tears
And cherubs appear in holy fire.

The peace in heaven's steadfast beat,
God gives me the here and now,
He sets a sign in those northern skies,
I see the seven stars of my plough.

Stonemason's Nightmare

A stonemason chipped away at a gargoyle
On the church in form of a dragon's head,
Surprised when his spirit sighed and groaned,
Found he could feel a presence of the dead.

How this creature seemed to be able to control
His hammer and chisel in his other hand,
When thoughts from the past entered his mind,
Way back in those days in old England.

After he tucked himself in bed that night,
He tossed and turned throughout his nightmare
About that fiery fiend who flew down to prey
Upon the village Saint Michaelmas fair.

Inside a pavilion he saw a group of monks,
Stuffing and gorging themselves with roasted goose,
Washed down with tankards of mead and far too merry
To heed his warning a dragon was on the loose.

He pleaded with musicians plucking their lutes,
Sitting there in winkle picker shoes,
He shouted at the people in pied piper hats,
Dancing round and round on the green in twos.

He saw the dragon rear up on his hind legs,
And stood well back from his blazing breath,
That smelt like burning brimstone and rotten eggs,
And bodies littered the village green with death.

There on his knees he prayed to Almighty God,
Relieved he sent Saint Michael his archangel,
In shining armour bearing a shield and sword,
Then struck it like fury, that fiend up from hell.

His answered prayer filled him with much delight,
Now the dragon was bound, it shrieked and hissed,
Saw Saint Michael hurl him with all his might,
How it roared all the way into the abyss.

Ringing church bells stirred him the next morning,
And he awoke shaking from his nightmare,
But glad to see the king and his retinue,
Come to the village Saint Michaelmas fair.

Cross Hill

A labourer forged his way to his fen cottage,
Cursed the bitter wind and swirling snow,
Till at last he lifted up his door latch,
How he welcomed the warm firelight's glow.
He couldn't escape those thoughts in the icy blast,
That nagged and tormented him and took their toll,
The fear that disturbed him from the distant past
Just felt like that kettle about to boil.

He noticed his pregnant wife's worried look,
Wondered about that log he'd found at Cross Hill,
Laying there, drying inside his inglenook,
Its awesome presence seemed to freeze his will.
He feared the effect upon his unborn child,
After he listened to her talk about this bloke
In her bad dream, nailed to a wooden cross,
That ghost she saw in a dark red, hooded cloak.

He never forgot that time at Cross Hill;
That day he wandered in the fenland fog,
The spectre he saw out the corner of his eye,
When he stooped to pick up that pitch black log;
During the evening he heaved it on his fire,
Where those burning red coals blazed so bright,
He heard a scream inside the crackling flames;
Spat some sparks and caught his rug alight.

Later he fell half asleep in his rocking chair,
Saw sour faces in those glowing embers,
Startled when an evil red imp jumped out
Of the fire and followed by his members.

He realised these horned creatures rose out of hell,
The stench of brimstone stifled the cottage air,
That lulled him into an even deeper sleep,
And found he'd drifted into a nightmare.

This haunting took him back to the Celtic era,
Came to a place where time had frozen still,
Where he mingled with some Roman soldiers
Gathered together on the top of Cross Hill,
Gazed like ghouls at this Briton nailed to a cross,
He pitied this suffering victim, who looked so wan,
Saw how it filled his fellowmen with woe,
At the cruelty inflicted on this dying man.

Revenge seized his heart, and watched this woman
In black poison the soldiers' steaming broth,
Glad to see them staggering around in pain,
The way the troubled Britons showed their wrath
And struck all the drowsy men down dead,
He was so grieved this death caused so much ill,
At the fiend who stirred up all this evil,
Now the streams of blood ran down Cross Hill

He awoke and fire had consumed his log of oak,
Heard three loud knocks and opened his door,
Faced that ghost in his dark red, hooded cloak,
Disappeared in the wind with a roar,
And his red imps followed him full of scorn,
Spat out sulphur, pierced the air with screams.
Later that night his baby boy was born,
His eerie stigmata had shattered his dreams.

The Carpenter

Charlie was a carpenter by trade,
All sorts of things his hands had made;
He'd always been a man of vision,
Yet felt his soul was shackled in prison.
He went to unlock the church door,
Found he faced his task with awe,
He carved a figure, there on the pew,
Moment by moment his tension grew.
His figure became the Celtic Green Man,
That came to life by work of his hands.
He heard footsteps come down the nave,
Voices whisper deep from the grave,
He'd tapped the mediaeval mind,
Began to think what else he'd find.

That afternoon he felt so good,
Gazing in wonder at the ancient rood,
He worked upon the figure of Christ,
And he thought about his sacrifice.
He carved his features out with skill,
And he felt him move his will,
That crown of thorns upon his head;
The way his open wounds had bled,
He asked the Saviour to forgive his sin,
And make his heart be pure within.
His spirit now set free from prison,
Saviour gave him a new vision,
He closed the church's creaking door,
Quite soon he felt his spirit soar.

The Thatcher

Samuel was a Suffolk man at heart,
Who'd craved to be a thatcher since he was four,
He hitched his pair of horses onto his cart;
And he filled it with his bundles of straw.

How he loved his Lavenham in the vale,
Seemed as though he'd stepped right back in time,
When passing timbered houses, along its streets,
Whistling his Suffolk songs, that came to mind.

He worked his way up the roof from its eaves,
Laying his bundles of straw, stripped off his shirt,
Then pegged the straw with split hazel wood,
He shaped that ridge, to finish off his work.

He stood back from the cottage with roving eye,
And saw the sun light up his golden thatch,
Set against the summer's bright blue sky,
Saw smooth red roses, as a perfect match.

Now Sam had heard about the bare fist fights,
That afternoon went down to Lavenham fair,
He stripped right down to his waist, stood in the ring;
Fought with skill and beat the best man there.

That evening he drank his bitter at the Bull and Calf,
And walked into a fight with gentleman Jim,
Sam found his fancy footwork, too good by half;
Jim was knocked out with a right to his chin.

He rode his way back home in his horse and cart;
Turned and gave a glance from the brow of the hill,
His sense of pride welled up within his heart,
To see the cottage he'd thatched with craftsman's skill.

The Wheelwright

Walter worked for years as a wheelwright,
There in his workshop along by Pedlars Path,
He stuttered, slow of speech and given to spite,
But not a better man you'd find at his craft,
Sometimes he drank a pint in the Crowing Cock,
He often finished up being a laughing stock.

His spokes in his hub looked like a Catherine wheel,
Shaped and worked the wooden edge all round.
He clasped his wheel with a red hot ring of steel,
Waited a while and wheeled it along the ground,
Admired the strength that lay at centre hub,
Symmetry of those spokes, inspired from above.

Around midday he rested his weary limbs,
Read through chapter six from the Book of Isaiah,
He thought about being cleansed from his sins,
That heat from burning coals in his forge fire,
Saw a seraph appear, who burned in gold;
Stood and watched his mighty wings unfold.

His workshop shook; he saw incense smoke,
He heard the Lord speak through the seraph's voice,
His simple soul welled up in faith and hope,
Knew when a sinner repents the heavens rejoice,
He felt the glory of God and fell down in awe,
Saw that seraph rise through heaven's door.

Haunted Watermill

There at a haunted watermill,
Its dripping wheel went round and round,
That made a creaking rumbling sound,
Way up the river near Hangman's Hill.

Its granite stones, that crushed until
Many grains of corn were ground,
There at a haunted watermill;
Its dripping wheel went round and round.

Sacks of flour have had their fill,
Workmen's hearts began to pound,
See that ghostly miller who drowned;

His presence left an icy chill,
There at a haunted watermill,
Its dripping wheel went round and round.

The Cobbler

By day a cobbler sat in his shop,
Shaping soles with his leather knife,
He listened to his ticking clock
And thought about his tragic life,
A cripple ever since he was born,
All full of bitterness and scorn.

He read his books by lantern light,
Studied for many a late hour,
Found his knowledge reached its height,
Now he'd gained this psychic power.
Opened his door, welcomed an elf,
He used his magic to glorify self.

Next day he met the elves of earth,
Cracked up, when he stumbled and fell,
He learnt their language, mischief and mirth,
Then went on to astral travel,
Understood ancient rites from the past,
Now he'd removed nature's mask.

Deep in the heart of an ancient forest,
He walked in a dried-up riverbed,
Came to treasure among some barrows,
There beneath a dragon's head,
He fled from its burning brimstone breath,
That almost frightened him to death.

Later he came to ancient Britain,
Here at the pagan feast of Beltane.
He joined a circle of chanting Druids,
Watched those fires all burst into flame,
That roared like hell's red fiery furnace,
Those future horrors he'd have to face.

Tinker

Stinging nettles grew round Fred's old shed,
Where his pitch black bulldog stood guard,
There among the kettles, pots and pans,
All littered around his yard.

How his temper weighed so heavy on his heart;
After every few words he swore.
He limped along beside his horse and cart
And he went from door to door.

A witch's copper kettle caught him unaware,
When his hammer struck his thumb,
Saw a red horned imp that made him swear,
Who kicked him hard and bit his bum.

Burly tinker's face went red with rage,
Fell backwards in a puddle of mud,
Furious the yokels all cracked up with laughter,
When he found this fiend drew blood.

He set his ferocious dog on the old hag,
Her wicked curse, struck it down dead,
He sat and howled, just like a troubled child,
Broken, went straight back home to bed.

Heaps of metal whizzed around in the air,
Crashed and banged all through the night,
Evil spirits entered every room,
The poor old man died in fright.

Tailor

A little tailor sat there sewing
At his bench, in his village shop,
He had a visit from an elfin king,
Right on stroke of six o'clock,
He watched him jump around in glee;
Then he bowed before His Majesty.

He measured cloth for King's red gown,
Expecting to receive a hoard of gold,
Asked him where it could be found;
There in a wood, beyond the wold,
The royal replied, with a taunting laugh,
Furious he chased him up the path.

Early next morning he left the village,
Walked beside a winding stream,
Crossed over a pack horse bridge,
And met the elfin King and Queen,
Came to the place, where he'd been told,
There in a wood, beyond the wold.

Among white-spotted red toadstools,
He stepped into a fairy ring,
Right where kingdom of darkness rules,
He stooped and robed the elfin king,
Saw him disappear in a blinding flash,
But found his gold beneath the ash.

Soldier

Frank, a redcoat soldier, loved to hear
The sound of a thousand soldiers' marching feet,
Advancing in ranks, through a battlefield,
In time with the kettledrum's rolling beat.

Early in the dark red dawn, he marched on,
Listening to those Scottish bagpipes roar,
Until his sense of glory rose in the clouds,
He'd fight like a hero in this bloody war.

Soon he reached the top of a grassy bank,
Saw a hundred cannons flash and flare,
And he felt unsteady on his feet,
Now cannonballs whistled through the air.

Thick black clouds of smoke made him choke
And he rubbed his eyes, that started to smart,
Wished the earth would swallow him up,
Found he couldn't control his thumping heart.

He heard a bugler sound the cavalry charge,
Their horses' hooves all thudded like thunder,
Watched the cavalry's sabres flash like lightning,
Split the entire Frenchmen's ranks asunder.

Sailor

Samuel sails those Arctic seas,
Fights with wind and waves,
Surging water soaks the deck,
Howling tempest raves.

Frost soon glistens on his beard,
Coldness threatens his life,
Flakes of snow all whiten his ship,
Icy wind cuts like a knife.

When his nerves become all strained,
Ropes and rigging taut
Snap in two under tension,
Now he's overwrought.

Dripping sailor sways on deck,
Grabs the spinning helm,
Drunken ship goes round and round,
Here in the Devil's realm.

Then his heart sinks fifty fathoms,
Sees that serpent's head
Breathe its flames of streaming fire;
It fills his soul with dread.

Cobwebs form in freezing fog,
Time to ring the bell,
Crippled ship creaks and groans,
Demons haunt him from hell.

Sailing on his skeleton ship
With a wounded heart,
Finds he's drifting in despair,
And tears himself apart.

Rich Man

Earl Grey entered the gates to his stately home,
Between the griffins, set on pillars of stone,
He wore a stylish coat, in satin black;
A diamond sparkled upon his white cravat,
With powdered wig and bow, that looked so neat;
He wore a small patch high upon his cheek.
He walked along his path, in stately pride,
His body movements betrayed his darker side,
Swinging his silver-knobbed swagger stick,
Enjoyed a string quartet's soothing music.
He took a waiting lady upon his arm;
Amused her with his polished wit and charm,
Admiring her heaving bosom and slender waist,
He watched her footsteps, gliding along in grace.
At night he watched fireworks light up the sky,
Enhanced his garden, lifted his soul on high.
His soul found solace and order in classical style,
Demons clouded his dreams that proved so vile,
Their deathly presence made him feel afraid,
Confirmed his fears about his masquerade.

He walked beside a fountain's soaring spray;
Moonlight beams silvered his garden pathway,
He smelt cascading flowers from Grecian urns,
Flowering blossom, whichever way he turned.
He looked like the Devil appearing as angel of light,
Wearing his stylish coat in satin white;
With matching waistcoat, embroidered in gold brocade,
He wore his mask there for the masquerade.
Under an arch of roses, he turned to his left,
Between some balustrades, onto stone steps,

Entered the ballroom, his heart quickened in pace;
He met the depths of his soul there, face to face.
The polished black-and-white chequered floor,
Mozart's music made his spirit soar,
He watched the glowing candles in chandeliers,
All sparked in red, in green and violet tears.
He joined masked ladies and gentlemen in dance,
His eighteenth century manner all enhanced.
During a dance he felt the chequered floor shake,
Saw the candles blow out, like a birthday cake,
Chandeliers all played a Chinese scale,
Earl and all his guests went deathly pale,
When he removed his mask at midnight and met
With faces, that turned to white skulls of death.

Poor Man

Peter went poaching in Hangman's Wood,
He listened to an owlet's cries,
Moved around as quiet as he could,

Beneath those cloudy moonlit skies,
Sensed a presence, quickened his step,
Saw the ghostly gamekeeper's eyes.

He felt him breathing down his neck;
Quickened his pace, until he ran,
Found he broke out all in a sweat.

He stopped in his tracks and made a stand,
Then he heard a sudden snap,
He bellowed out in pain, poor man,

And found his ankle was caught in a trap.

Beggar Man

The beggar man stared in his wooden bowl,
He sat till evening beside a road,
That led into a haunted drove.

He shook his bowl, all troubled in soul,
Hoping someone would lighten his load,
The beggar man stared in his wooden bowl.

His soul glowed like a lump of coal;
Found his thoughts began to rove,
Dreaming of finding a treasure trove,
The beggar man stared in his wooden bowl.

Thief

William left the Queen of Hearts,
One night in late October,
He sauntered down a lamp-lit street;
Seemed he was barely sober.

About half a mile down the road,
When he came to Earl Grey's estate,
Walked by the high red-bricked wall
And he fiddled with the gate.

He crept beneath a stately oak,
Disturbed a hooting owl,
Stopped in his tracks when he heard
Some foxhounds give a howl.

How he loved the garden's fountain,
Captured in the moonlight's glow,
Went up to the Georgian Mansion,
There in through the window.

Once inside, he gazed around
And felt a presence there,
Saw a ghostly Georgian lady
Come down a winding stair.

This made his dark hair stand on end,
He shook with nerves so raw,
Saw a sparkling emerald necklace,
Right there inside a drawer.

He felt the lady grip his hand,
Watched her remove her mask,
All full of fear he ran for his life,
Not able to face his task.

Sheet lightning flashed through the window,
When he ran down the hall;
Family portraits sneered at him,
That hung upon the wall.

Fenland Tales

These folk tales express the darkness of medieval times and invoke a sense of mystery, of both good and evil.

The ghostly monks in Ely Cathedral and the surrounding ancient abbeys are set in haunting landscape with its reeds and willows, and with will-o'-the-wisp moving over the dark face of its misty waters.

Night

Stars they twinkle overhead,
When young children sink in bed
And just before they go to sleep,
A book of fairy tales is read;
Believe every word that is said
That goes down in their souls so deep.

They hear a sandman's slouching feet,
Walking down the village street,
They dream of a magic crescent moon,
See some gathering pixies peep,
A huge giant lies down in a heap,
Dish runs away with his spoon.

They fly upon a witch's broom,
See the graveyard spirits loom,
Know where bogeymen are bred;
See them dance on an infant's tomb.
Children see shadows in their bedroom,
All their hearts are filled with dread.

Nun's Funeral Raft

I stood there fishing, plied my rod,
High on a bank in fenland fog,
I stared in the River Ouse that night,
Smelt those torches burning so bright
And a draught that flickered each flame,
Lit up the funeral raft in shame,
Six monks knelt down there in prayer,
Their hoods created a haunting air.
I froze in fear, right where I stood,
When each monk turned his drooping hood,
Their huge eyes glowed, so red and wild;
Their white skulls gave an evil smile.
I found my heaving heart soon sank,
Saw those monks moor on the bank,
Beneath that cathedral, up the hill
They carried the nun in midnight chill,
All under a curse of eternal death,
Spoke Latin, from their frosty breath.
I watched them finger their rosary beads,
And heard the sound of jangling keys
Unlock an oak cathedral door,
Their torches lit that stone cold floor.
I followed them and came to a halt,
Watched the nun laid down in her vault.

King Canute's Visit to Ely

Canute's ship sailed near the Isle of Ely,
His crew was pulling on its creaking oars,
He heard some monks singing in the abbey
On Candlemas, that made his spirit soar.

He listened to the abbey's piercing bell,
Seemed to heighten the sun's golden fire,
Sparkling on those frosty trees like angels,
That inspired his vision of a celestial choir.

His dragon ship went sailing, on and on,
His soldiers' oars were striking a steady beat,
Rowing south to a mere he came along,
Found where salt and fresh waters meet.

At evening the sun sank into the shade,
His bearded face was lit by torches' flames,
When voices from the abbey started to fade,
Fear began flowing through his veins.

He stared at frosty willows, that looked so crisp,
Cobwebs hung down from a frozen reed bed.
Tongues of blue fire from the will-o'-the-wisp,
Those tormented spirits of the Saxon dead.

His ship sailed farther and farther into the unknown,
Fog was steaming, like a witch's cauldron,
Something slimy in the water glowed
And he faced a forty-foot demon.

He'd sailed in the spirit world and lost at night,
Swirling mist had caused his heart to freeze,
His fingers, raw from a touch of frostbite,
How he cursed that cruel north-easterly breeze.

Images haunted him mile after mile,
Shivering there on board in the winter's chill,
Till at last he moored his ship on the Isle
And burning torches lit his way uphill.

Later he opened the abbey's groaning door,
Saw some candles flickering all around.
Eerie monks now filled his heart with awe,
Then he fell down flat on hallowed ground

When he saw their skulls in drooping hoods
Chanting words in Latin that sounded so devout,
This sacred music invoked a presence of death,
That shocked him when the candles all snuffed out.

Denny Abbey

Darkness came down that moonlit night in Denny Abbey,
Where Templars held secrets
   God forbade them all to know,
Spoke the words from an ancient scroll
   that possessed a key

To unlock the power that caused this evil wind to blow,
As they stood in the zodiac on a white stone floor,
There in a circle of twelve black candles flickering low.

Stirred by dragons, flying through the open door,
Swooped around them spewing out unholy fire,
Darted to and fro and made a deafening roar.

High in the vaulted roof they saw a ghostly choir
Of Benedictine monks, who chanted, 'Kyrie eleison,'
Inside the flames, blazing like a funeral pyre.

How they grieved about this inferno for so long,
When they heard the chiming from that midnight bell
And a devil prophesied on the coming Babylon.

They felt so furious they'd fallen under this demonic spell,
Met the grim-faced reaper whetting his deadly scythe,
And they choked on brimstone from the fires of hell.

Horrified, they fled outdoors seeking to hide,
Stepped on a raft and guided by a ferryman,
Saw Odin's yellow-eyed, black dog that never died,

Crouched in the frosty reeds and willows looking so wan,
Haunted by bluish lanterns from the will-o'-the-wisp,
The nagging sense of being watched wherever they ran.

Their bitterness worse than bogs that bubbled and hissed,
Dreaded the bony finger that pointed to endless pain,
Now realised their souls were on the brink of the abyss,

On this dark journey that proved to be a bane,
Began cursing from their icy clouds of breath,
As their ferryman pulled and pulled on the sagging chain,

Found they were on their way to face eternal death.

Candlemas

Grim Reaper sharpened his scythe, all ready to mow
A harvest of souls to a lost eternity
That led to hell's raging red fires below.

He forged his way through fog to Denny Abbey,
Stepped onto a ferry, in lantern's light,
On the black waters of this haunted sea.

He stepped ashore in the frosty moonlit night,
When the vespers bell chimed its tongue,
The time had come for his power to reach its height.

How he mocked that plainchant being sung,
His skeleton fingers opened the creaking door;
It froze the heart of every wary nun.

There in his drooping cowl, his face red raw;
He'd come to spread the evil Black Death
And made the demonic and evil spirits soar.

He blew so hard, with his fiery brimstone breath,
That stifled the air, and snuffed the candles out,
Vowed the grave would reign before he left.

He was so proud to bring this misery about,
Heard voices plead with Christ, through Mary's name,
Found he'd been cast in the arena of doubt.

Furious those smouldering candles burst into flame,
He collapsed into a heap of rags and dust;
Blew away in a wind and whined in pain.
Now the power of prayer had quenched his lust.

Spinney Abbey

A farmer lost his way in Wicken fen,
How he cursed that November night,
Growling ghosts and ghouls all taunted him,
That filled his restless heart with fright.

Once in his farmhouse at Spinney Abbey,
He bolted and barred his old oak door,
Heard some angry voices and rattling chains
Come from beneath his grey stone floor.

A presence made him freeze in the icy breeze,
That kept on flickering the candles' flames,
He slowly turned his head and fixed his gaze,
Saw three black canons there in chains.

He watched the canons sink down into hell,
Where a hundred devils laughed,
Surprised the wind died down outside his farm,
He heard footsteps along his path.

He met the canon's ghost there at his door,
His heart raced at a deadly pace,
At the Augustinian canon's evil,
A dropping black hood covered his face.

The frightened farmer shook, his blood ran cold,
He moved closer to his roaring fire,
Would the farmer ever forget that ghastly
Look on the face of the murdered prior?

He turned and saw the prior pointing his finger
Straight at the canon's bloodstained knife,
The farmer could hardly believe he'd met
With him who took the prior's life.

Ely Cathedral

That moment I opened the cathedral's door,
Smelt the musty walls of ancient stone,
I heard some hooded monks' strange voices soar.

I followed in their footsteps, all filled with awe,
Found my soul had flown to the unknown,
That moment I opened the cathedral's door.

I met a host of angels and demons at war,
My soul seemed trapped inside this timeless zone,
I heard some hooded monks' strange voices soar,

They swung their censers like never before,
Above I saw winged seraphs around a throne,
That moment I opened the cathedral's door,

Where I saw hell's fiery furnace roar;
My soul became filled with religion of Rome,
I heard some hooded monks' strange voices soar.

How I loathed the liturgy, this Latin lore,
Corpses down in the crypt began to groan,
That moment I opened the cathedral's door,
I smelt the musty walls of ancient stone.

Halloween

Ely Cathedral in heart of the fen,
Children who meet there at quarter to ten,
How their white innocent faces now smile,
Put on demonic black masks to beguile,
Lighting their pumpkins on Cathedral Green,
They're so possessed by this black Halloween,
Watching old hags ride their broomsticks so high,
Lit by the moon in a starry night sky,
Mischievous youngsters they trick and they treat,
Knocking on doors there along the dark street,
Meet with those princes and powers of the air,
Seen in the lightning, that gives them a scare.
They all soon find their spirits are marred,
Down on their way to the church's graveyard,
Dancing round graves with frosty white breath,
Feeling the presence from those demons of death,
Realise they're gripped now in death's cold embrace,
Wonder what other dark terrors they'll face.

Now they see lightning, hear thunderous roars,
When they all stare into hell's open jaws,
Feel the hot breath from this place so depraved,
Slip down the gullet to cathedral cave,
Burn in a belly that's raging with fire,
Choking on brimstone engulfed with desire,
Watching the demons, who wield lightning whips,
Scourging the damned in their smoking grey pits,
Children see flesh that is flayed to the bone,
Hark how they scream before Satan's dark throne.

Then they hear chimes from the cathedral's bell,
Striking midnight when they come out of hell,
Open the creaking cathedral oak door,
Meet hooded monks who soon fill them with awe,
Watching them singing their plainchant in Latin,
In their black cowls and their skulls with that grin,
Now that their haunted young souls are possessed,
Seek cathedral dark spirits that manifest,
Clouding their hearts like the misty black fen,
Meet the Green Man on this Celtic Samhain.
When they all find they're in death's vice-like grip,
Rousing dead bodies inside the grey crypt,
Find they're all dancing to pagan dark rites,
Ecstatic on this most wicked of nights.

They're so surprised by the bishop's old shrine,
Filling their spirits with love so divine,
Being so blessed by this saint from the past,
They all remove their demonic black masks,
Seeing the light streaming down from the Lamb,
Meet here with Jesus, the heavenly man.
Now they've been cleansed from this dark night of sin,
Feeling new innocence glowing within,
Singing with angels in blissful high heaven,
Wake up in cathedral round half past seven.
Stirred by the organ that shakes the stone floor
And the choirboys' high voices all echo and soar,
Children now celebrate on All Saints Day.
Praise Christ Jesus who lights their new way.

Witches of Wicken

Hark the chiming midnight bell,
Summon Prince of Power from hell,
I see him there in Devil's hall,
Makes the thunder flashes fall,
I hear some goblins grovel and growl,
Curse those hounds of hell that howl.
My spirit at one with Prince of Power,
There in hell this midnight hour.
Knights light up in flashing storm;
Hearken to their battle horn.
I watch them mount their skeleton steeds;
They breathe out their brimstone breeze.
Wait there on unhallowed ground,
Hear the drawbridge lowered down.
I see the hundreds of Valpurgis knights
Ride into the starry heights,
Where the heavens flash and flame;
In a storm that brings no rain,
Wield their glowing swords and shields,
Reflect like fire in the Wicken fields.
I hear the riders' horses' hooves
There above those moonlit roofs,
Thunder flashes in Wicken Fen,
Awake the ancient spirits and men,
And blue flame from will-o'-the-wisps
I hear them hiss at Valpurgis.
See these knights all gather round,
And wait to take the hallowed ground.

I guide the Prince and Power of the air,
Who's chosen a Wicken virgin so fair,

I see her presence brighten her way;
There in the middle of the day,
Walk across Maid's Head Green,
Her mincing steps so clearly seen;
Betray her heart so full of pride,
A sense of purity she cannot hide.
Her family curse she'll not escape;
Not her fortune, nor her fate,
I'll offer her as a sacrifice,
There in the summer solstice,
And ignite the power of ancient rites,
Raise those spirits on pagan sites.

From a cauldron glowing red hot;
I scrape my fingers inside the pot,
This powder dried from boiling broth,
I kindle in sparkling flames of wrath.
First I add an adder's tongue;
Mix with bits of dragon's dung,
Sprinkle with some seasonal herbs,
Stir with blood from newborn birds.
Toads once buried at Dragon's Green;
Their bones once moved and danced upstream.
Young bats' blood that's burned to a crisp,
That I silvered in moon's eclipse.
I throw this powder high in the air,
See the spirits flash and flare;
Casting my witch's magic spells,
Arouse the demons that dwell in hell.
I invite the ghoul, fiend and beast,
And greet them here at Wicken feast.

Last Day of April

A gang of children played hide and seek,
Down the bottom of Pedlar's Road,
Found their way through a farmer's field
They mimicked a cuckoo in the drove.

They stared at woolly clouds in heaven,
Morning sun sat smiling beyond,
Reflected like a golden sovereign,
Then watched it glare in the pond.

When those angry clouds went black,
They sat huddled together in a bower,
Screamed at a sudden clap of thunder,
All soaked by a short, sharp April shower.

They saw the sun pop out again,
That lifted those heavy clouds of doubt,
A glowing rainbow filled those skies,
Made them all give out a shout.

Naughty kids sneaked out that night,
They could hardly believe their eyes,
Watched the witches on besom brooms
Fly beneath the moonlit skies.

They scrambled through a hole in a fence
That led to a farmer's field beyond,
Saw the moon glow, like a sixpence,
There in the middle of Friars Pond.

A whining wraith scared them to death,
Knew this man had cut his throat,
They saw blood run through his whiskers,
That dripped onto his Sunday coat.

They dared to follow a ghostly sexton,
All heard him ring the old church bell,
Met ghouls among the mossy graves
And evil spirits that came from hell.

All the innocents turned and fled,
Chased by the howling bogeymen,
Along with phantoms, lantern-led,
Hot on the heels of spooked children.

The Meeting

A phantom that night on Halloween
Crossed some stones set in a stream;
There in his drooping hooded cloak,
His cloven hooves just like a goat,
He walked along a pilgrim's path,
And he struck it with his staff.
He heard the cathedral's chiming bell,
Shouted curses down a well,
Right near a cottage, beside a road
That led into a haunted drove;
Ruins of a priory looked so bleak,
This is where he was to speak;
Spirits he summoned were evil in form,
They flashed their wings upon the storm.

The Pedlar, the Witch and the Imp

Red imp who followed me one day,
I saw him behind the witch's door,
That day she sent him out to play.

I'm a pedlar, my name is Ray,
Nothing happened like this before,
Red imp who followed me one day.

It even led my thoughts astray,
Bedazzled by his evil lore,
That day she sent him out to play.

The imp jumped this way, that way,
Onto my chest, and how I swore,
When lying on my bed of hay.

Beside my bed I knelt to pray,
He glowed there on my bedroom floor,
Red imp who followed me one day.

I couldn't keep that thing at bay,
Wished him in hell, that's for sure,
Red imp who followed me one day,
That day she sent him out to play.

Rural and Village Life

This explores how it feels to experience the beauty in nature and the community spirit.

This is also reflected in historical Huntingdon through the Puritans' apocalyptic vision that eventually brought freedom to every citizen in this nation.

Joy of Christmas

Hoar frost covers hedges,
Hoar frost covers trees,
Children ride their sledges,
How their fingers freeze.

Mother's in the kitchen,
Making Christmas pud,
While her son and daughter
Bring holly from a wood.

Maids hang mistletoe
At the Tudor hall,
Go to lattice-window,
Watch the snowflakes fall.

Farther down the village,
Church that so inspires,
Hark the organ's playing,
Music sung by a choir.

In the Rose and Crown,
Folks all filled with cheer,
Sitting round a fire,
Drink their spirits and beer.

See those carol singers
Stand in lantern's glow,
Sing the season's tidings,
There in falling snow.

Spring

See the spring light falling,
Down on Meadow Green,
Hark the cuckoo's calling,
There in this country scene.

Dairymaids are walking,
Love those buttercup vales,
Farmers stand there talking;
Tell each other tales.

Soft May breezes blowing,
Breathe through Holm-Oak Hill,
Hedges' blossoms are glowing,
Nearby a watermill.

Pretty girls are playing,
Skip down country lanes,
Sit in meadows maying,
Make their daisy chains.

Rooks and crows are cawing,
There above their nests,
Spend time wheeling, soaring,
Then come down to rest.

Village church bells ringing,
Fill the springtime air,
Happy children are singing;
Make their way to a fair.

Short-eared bats are flying,
Dart there to and fro,
Now the twilight's dying,
Moon is half aglow.

Long-eared owls are hooting;
Barely blink their eyes,
Twinkling stars, some shooting,
Fill the springtime skies.

Springtime

Green banks are laced with golden daffodils,
Hyacinths scent the cottage windowsills,
Children rolling about, head over heels,
Leapfrog and jump, over the rushing rills,
Chase, capture and court those springtime thrills,
Heighten their spirits, to what their nature feels.

Right in the heart of a village, a church bell peals,
Sound of a pedlar's horse and clattering cartwheels,
Morris dancers are on the village green,
Jingling their bells when doing their foursome reels,
Shepherds hold their crooks and toil in the fields,
Near where a host of newborn lambs are seen.

A milkmaid sells her freshly made cream,
Dreams of being crowned the garland may queen.
She walks in the evening, hears the skylark's trills,
In flowery meadows caught in a sunlit gleam
As she skips along by a weaving stream,
That leads down to the quaintest of watermills.

Fairy Wedding

A fairy princess courts her king,
Makes sweet music on the wing,
Flies in blossom's bright red hue,
Sits on a sprig and starts to sing,
Shares the joys their love will bring,
Hears birds whistle their love song too.

There on a bank of violets blue,
She listens to the crafty cuckoo,
Spreads her golden wings in flight,
Watches the red sun peeping through,
Shines on her clothes that glisten like dew,
Now lands in those meadows of delight.

Among the lady's smock so white
She trips along by Devil's Dyke,
Comes to a glowing fairy ring,
Wears her crown all sparkling bright,
And on this perfect moonlit night
She celebrates this royal wedding.

Twilight Time

Now the twilight starts to turn,
Deadly nightshade lanterns burn,
Glowing yellow and deep purple,
See the moths begin to circle.
Short-eared bats dart overhead,
Wake the spirits of the dead,
Lying low in garden's glade,
Rise to life and thrive in shade.
Spirits begin to weave their spells,
Hover over bubbling wells,
Fairies and elves begin to play,
End this bright midsummer's day.

Time for mischief, time for fun,
Now those bees no longer hum,
Now the dark and evil rules,
Elves emerge from toadstools,
Hear that hooting tawny owl,
Makes the farmer's hounds all howl,
Under moon just like a slither,
Spirits emerge from the river,
Underground springs and wells,
Every nature spirit excels.

Huntingdon

Huntingdon, the shire's mother town,
And she births its passion and Puritan fire,
With a divine purpose that toppled a crown,
When civil war in Britain seemed so dire,
Canon balls dented many a mansion,
Simple farmers, tillers of the soil,
Heard the rampant Lion roar from Zion,
Attacked what the nation considered royal.
King Charles the First, promoter of classical culture,
His Cavaliers so full of idolatry,
Preyed on people like a starving vulture,
Loved oppression, despised democracy.
Cromwell proved diligent in his search,
Smote the Green Man and whitewashed walls,
Covered the murals in the Catholic Church.
He pictures that time when the Antichrist falls.
Disciplined Roundheads felt God's heartbeat,
Holy Spirit pulsating through their veins,
Through this military machine's marching feet
And proclaiming, "The Lord Almighty reigns!"
Moving through the land like dawn arising,
Soldiers bowed their heads so deep in prayer,
Looked up to the clouds to the coming King,
For the presence of Jesus filled the air,
Now feel that force of His kingdom power,
Cromwell's sword of the Spirit high in his hand,
Triumphant through Christ in his finest hour,
That offered freedom for every man in England.

A Stroll Around Houghton

On the way to rustic Houghton,
Through the thicket's shady lane,
Passing by the old vicarage,
Ghostly stare from window pane.
On stormy nights the Rector's face
Darkens and haunts unwary souls,
When the flashing lightning strikes
And the clapping thunder rolls.

Now it's time to move along,
Click your heels and double back,
Flowery fields are filled with song,
Walking on well-trodden track
On the bank of old age Ouse,
Gazing at those Hemingford Spires,
Take in first class rural views,
Georgian mansion so inspires.
Boats are chugging down the river,
Sun picks up their glistening wake,
Makes the water's edges shiver,
See the widening ripples break.

Cross a bridge above a weir,
Take a journey back in time,
On the train through Huntingdonshire,
Puffing along the railway line,
On this most memorable trip,
Moving through this springtime day,
Carriages going clickety-click,
Clickety-click and fade away.

Stepping on a new wooden bridge,
Where willows fall like golden rain,
Toadstools form an elfin village,
Fairy faces all aflame.
Turn around and follow stream,
Fish dart through the water so clear,
Over the rocks in silvery gleam,
Watch the fairy queen appear.

Stare at those majestic trees,
Mirrored in the water so still;
Stop for cream and afternoon teas
On picnic tables by Houghton Mill,
Waters tread the dripping wheel,
Grinding granite jaws devour,
Rumbling with unyielding zeal,
Sacks are being filled with flour.
Phantom Rector opens gate
Between the church's crumbling wall,
Drifting on, all filled with hate,
With his spirit as bitter as gall,
Here he meets eternal death,
Making demons rant and rave,
Smells the rising brimstone breath
Coming from a blacksmith's grave,
Sees his forge's fire ablaze,
Hears his hammer ring the anvil,
Choking on the smoke and haze,
There on his way to the flames in hell.

Oh, to see the May sun shine
On the streets of crooked cottages!
People mass around the clock tower,
Right near The Three Jolly Butchers.
Maidens dancing around the maypole,
Coloured ribbons interlace;
Fires up passions within each soul
In ritual dance that's gathering pace,
Bare white feet beating on ground,
See how the springtime spirit glows,
Girls are swishing round and round
Till their psychic energy flows,
Rising like a gushing fountain,
Here in the happy heart of Houghton.

Holywell

Village church is mounted on a hill
With its swinging merry bells ringing
Over leaning graves so peaceful and still.

Steep stone steps lead to a bubbling spring,
Coins all glittering in this Holywell,
Place for pilgrim, saint and Celtic king;

Gracing visitors with their timeless spell,
Standing on this site of hallowed ground,
Touches where the deepest feelings dwell,

Medieval monks' low voices sound,
Plainchant coming from this sacred shrine,
Weeping willow hangs like bishop's gown,

Garland well impresses on the mind,
Stirs distant rituals from the past,
Here on this journey way back in time.

When the Britons wear blue woad and mask,
Dance before red-bearded sun at Beltane,
With their frenzied feet and mouths aghast,

Druids stand near bonfires all aflame,
Blood now soaks the sacred altar stone,
Pretty virgin screaming out in pain,

Everywhere the evil spirits roam,
Fresh spring waters surging up so bright,
Harpists, pipers' notes enhance the tone.

Heightens nature in this religious rite,
Brings out music from every flower,
Emerald meadows sparkling with delight.

Now the air immersed with psychic power,
All the souls now reach a feverish pitch,
Darker side of nature seeks to devour.

Magic spoken by a hooded witch,
Making underground horned demons rave,
Set in sequence in this solar eclipse,

Over the earth like a giant black wave.
Fuel its energies so deep below,
Send its terrors from beyond the grave.

Present day thatched white cottages in a row,
There on the bank of this Saxon ring hamlet,
With their gardens in the evening's glow

Fading in the darkening red sunset,
Swarming short-eared bats' squeaky din,
Darting just above the ghostly Juliet,

Gliding on the road to the Ferry Boat Inn,
Stepping onto the craft, lantern-led,
Faces the ferryman, looking so grim,

Go to a land where hopes and dreams have fled.

Holywell

The new Saint Ivian mayor rises at dawn,
In this glorious month of May,
Purple and dark red clouds all clothe this morn,
Glossy buttercups brighten her way.
When the sun begins peeping through,
She listens to the trilling lark,
Birds' liquid notes in time with cuckoo,
Woodpecker tapping on the bark,
She adores the weeping willow leaves so quaint
That dangle in the River Ouse.
She follows in the path of Persian Saint,
Watches the wake from boats that cruise,
All those lofty trees that girdle Houghton Hill,
Beneath the soaring grey church spires,
How this gives her spirit such a thrill,
In the Hemingford meadow that fires
Her up on a road to the bridge chapel,
Where smells from town tickle her nose,
Welcomed by the chiming church bells;
Fill her with joy, wherever she goes;
She walks so sprightly on the stone-paved quay,
Passes the Victorian lampposts,
Stares across the waters to the lea,
Here in haunts of the river-port ghosts.
Later she opens a major event in town,
Stands in the crowd looking so grand,
In three-cornered hat and bright red gown,
Before the Somersham brass band;
Under Cromwell's statue and church steeple,
She presides with her usual flare,
Looking so traditional among the people.
Make way for new Saint Ivian mayor!

Carnival month in hot baking July,
She hears the sound of marching feet,
Military men, all capture her eye,
Move in step along the street.
How she loves to hear their kettledrums roll,
Hair stands up on the back of her hand,
Bagpipes roar, touch the depths of her soul,
Heightened by the blazing brass band;
She throws her coins into rattling pails,
Faces the firemen dressed in drag,
Amused by their grins behind flimsy veils,
Their balloon boobs pop from a red hot fag.
Next she sees the local beauty queens,
Wearing their coloured silk sashes,
Sitting together in their land of dreams,
Throw kisses, with fluttering eyelashes.
She's so impressed with many passing floats,
Laughs at the characters that rant and rail,
So pleased to see one of her favourite soaps,
And that theme tune from Emmerdale.
First she judges the floats on Hill Rise Park,
Then listens to pop groups twanging guitars,
And in the night retains her traditional spark.
She sits under the dome of the stars,
So stunned by music's heavy beat and rhythm,
Taken in by its haunting tone,
Finds she's drawn into hell's deep chasm,
There in a place where devils roam.
She feels a presence of death and starts to shake,
So wrapped up in unholy sound,
That the heavens and earth seem to vibrate
And sees dark forces over the town,

Then fountains of fireworks fall like golden rain,
Startling her being with delight,
Seeing the vaults of heaven set aflame,
Where her spirit reaches its height,
When those whizzing rockets go up and zoom
Into the air with a flash and a flare,
Exploding, echoing with an almighty boom,
They're crackling around everywhere.

Late September in the centre of Saint Ives,
She turns up at Saint Michaelmas Fair,
Sets the mood beneath those autumn skies,
With her distinctive traditional air,
Faces the crowds of people who stand aside,
From her man who bears the mace,
She upholds her authority with pride,
There in her sparkling golden necklace.
She's walking so stately in ceremonial dress,
Commands a respect from the distant past,
Her dignitaries in procession two abreast,
See these ancient customs still last;
There in all the sounding marching footsteps,
She hears Ivo's cries from the deep,
Reaching dizzy heights and down to depths,
Once touched the heart of Saxon Slepe.
She loves that moment when children rally round,
Rolling their pennies, amidst the laughter,
Yet she enforces the 'no go' area in town,
In obedience with the Royal Charter,

When she gazes at the spire church clock,
Time to open the Saint Michaelmas fair;
She's deafened by the beat from heavy rock,
That vibrates across the market square.
She's dazzled by those coloured flashing lights,
As she goes round on the big wheel,
Here she reaches and enjoys the sights,
Embracing the town's youthful zeal,
Thoughts and ideas hammer through her brain,
For she's touched so many lives,
Barely halfway through her yearly reign,
Here in this town of Saint Ives.

Cambridge in the Twenties

How we treasured that grand May Ball,
Remembered when we turned and smiled,
Your rattling beads, your face went red,
When we danced the Charleston so wild;
We soon enhanced the swinging twenties,
Sipping our glasses of bubbling champagne,
And when the jazz band slowed the tempo,
Those tender magic moments came,
Balloons and streamers floated down,
There was no need for us to speak,
We finished up in a warm embrace;
There we danced cheek to cheek,
Touched upon our deepest desire,
When fireworks whizzed on high,
Sprinkling stars and fountains of fire
That lit the glorious Cambridge sky.

We punted along the river Granta,
How we loved this summery scene,
Flocks of sheep in Grantchester meadows,
We glided through those tunnels of green.
I wore my boater, white shirt and trousers,
Lifted and pushed my punting pole,
While you lazed inside the punt,
There under your shady parasol.
We moored the punt that afternoon,
Time had come for honey and tea;
Later we swam in Byron's pool,
Then we punted back to the city,

Under the wooden humpbacked bridge
By the red-bricked building of Queen's,
Came to the splendour of King's College
And found fulfilment in our dreams.

The Fox

He's a loner and mean;
Looks so hungry and lean,
Glossy coat so red,
There in burrow bred,
He's so rarely seen.

Round a field of sheep,
Foxy begins to creep,
Much too clever by half;
Uses cunning craft,
Makes that sudden leap.

Fox's running at dawn,
Hears the hunter's horn,
Hounds sniffing for blood,
Huntsmen's horses thud,
Thunder like a storm.

Fox's leaps and bounds,
Chased by barking hounds,
Under a reddening sun,
Ends his frightening run,
There in horrific sounds.

The Vagrant

I stepped right off that roundabout of life,
Claimed my patch upon the dark grey pavement,
All wrapped in newspaper in my cardboard home,
And slept with vagrants and shared their grief.
I lived under a heavy cloud of darkness,
Gambling led me down this road of despair,
Driven by power and greed that promised all;
Here in this cul-de-sac I found nothing
But handouts that fed this living death.
I spent a spell in a dingy dropout centre,
Managed to rid myself from drug addiction,
Saved some coins from my beggar's bowl,
Enough money to revisit my student days,
To search for my long-lost years in Cambridge.

Next day I went to a down-and-outs' hostel;
Spruced myself up in a second hand suit,
Gazed in the mirror, captured something of
My former self, but looked so thin and pale;
I faced my life, with haversack on my back,
Attempted to hitch a lift along the road;
I cursed the ceaseless flow of busy traffic,
Found I'd rolled down a steep embankment.
How I loved the smell of grass in the meadow,
Greeted by a blackbird's merry tune,
I heard the Almighty speak through his notes;
My heart began to feel at one with creation,
And I drank from a nearby bubbling spring.
I stumbled onto a broken grey milestone,
Looked up and saw some bleached branches of
An oak, covered with scores of black crows.

A shadow of my dark side had beckoned me,
I made my way straight through a cobwebbed hedge,
Found several huge green Saxon barrows.
I saw a crowd of dwarfs come out of a cave,
Grasping some sparkling Saxon jewellery,
Bracelets, necklaces and purses in red and blue,
Those ancient treasures delighted my greedy heart.
A large red dragon appeared breathing his fire,
Lifted me with his talons straight down to hell,
Where I was chained upon a revolving spit,
Roasted over a screaming pit of terror,
Where brimstone and flames spitted their hate;
There I woke all soaked in sweat at midnight.

I fled across some fields all filled with fear,
Drawn into the medieval mind;
Superstition set in, I saw dead spirits
That lurked there in the long moonlight shadows.
I saw some witches dancing around a bonfire,
All worshipped demons hovering in the air.
I ventured no farther and crossed a running stream,
For miles those chanting old hags haunted my soul.
I came to ruins of an old monastery,
A full moon shone right through its grey arches;
Ivy wrapped around the sacred stone.
I lay before the altar in the sanctuary,
Felt so shut away from the outside world;
I smelt incense and candles scent the air,
Heard some ghostly monks singing in Latin,
And I was struck by the glory of everything.

At dawn I arose and made for the motorway,
After my peace the traffic shattered my nerves.
Somehow I'd come to a busy service station,
Treated myself to a full English breakfast;
I drank several cups of fresh ground coffee.
The wheel of fortune was about to favour me,
And I met a chap who offered me a lift;
I dozed for many miles on the car journey,
Heard when wheels of the car soon ground to a halt.
I breathed in fresh Cambridge air, so thrilled
To knock upon my old professor's door.

That evening I wandered around Wandlebury;
Enjoyed those sights from Gog-Magog hills.
I went straight through the corridors of time,
Past events were glowing crystal clear,
I felt a direct link with ancient Druids,
And nature's forces from their fertility rites.
I found myself among the Celtic Chieftains,
All dressed in purple, blue and scarlet cloaks;
I was dazzled by their brooches and golden torcs.
I stood and watched their tribe in painted masks,
Watched them dancing round those Beltane fires.
I followed the Druids, who gathered in a circle,
Heard them pleading, then chant in Celtic tongues;
Summoned a giant warrior spirit, Wandil,
To fight against that evil demon of darkness
Who cast a shadow over the horn-shaped moon.
I saw Wandil appear, wielding his sword,
White magic fought against black magic,
And the demon of darkness was defeated.

Then I saw a strange giant-beaked horse
And sun god with Gog, blazing in his chariot;
Magog appeared upon her white horse.
I saw the moon now freed; it shone in glory
Over the age-old hills in Celtic Britain.

I punted so smoothly down the river Granta,
Found myself in Cambridge that May morning.
Memories of Emma flashed into my mind;
Her rosy face, blue eyes and golden tresses,
Lying before me wearing a long white dress,
Dangled her slender fingers into the water;
I knew these waters had passed under the bridge,
But couldn't stop thinking about my first real love.
Everywhere seemed like a new creation,
Those flowery paths, gardens and fresh green lawns,
Running on either side of the willowy banks;
King's College soared in a Cambridge blue sky.

Never will I forget that summer evening,
Seeing her arrayed in her evening ball gown,
Walking over the famous Bridge of Sighs,
Through cobbled courts to the grand May Ball.
Found myself in a marquee on a lawn,
I danced with her and went outside to watch
The fireworks whizzing high into the skies,
Burst like shooting stars and spokes of a wheel.
Later this moment turned to a bad nightmare,
When she expressed her desire to be a nun;
Ran away and I've never seen her since.

Reality struck and I dropped my punting pole,
It seemed she'd vanished like some fairy queen;
Things went from bad to worse, I fiddled around
My pockets in vain, unable to find my wallet;
Now broke, poverty came upon me like a thief.
Earlier I'd learned my professor had died,
Now homeless I had to doss down for the night.
I wrapped myself in a couple of dark grey blankets
And I slept beneath some stairs in St John's.
How I tossed and turned throughout the night,
I heard faint footsteps coming down the steps;
Found I'd met with ghost of a former doctor,
Beckoned me with his finger to his room,
Doctor Death was written above his door.
I stepped inside and saw shelf upon shelf
Of thousands of books on human philosophy,
I watched him standing there in cap and gown,
Inviting me into his Master's study to learn
Sophistry, black is white and white is black.
I recoiled and he faded in the realms of time,
He'd left me with a lack of meaning in life,
There were no yesterdays or tomorrows,
I began to curse abstract and rational thoughts,
Hegal's ideas taught in the universities,
That threatened the nature of every man's soul.

Next day I went down to the shopping centre,
Found the buskers' music lifted my spirits,
I tossed my last few coins in a crumpled coat,
Felt sorry for a man sitting with his dog.

I came to some Irishmen drinking meths,
Standing behind a long, white marble seat,
Oblivious to crowds of people walking by,
Going in and out of the busy library;
I learnt the ropes from those drunken dropouts,
Told where I could relieve my hunger.

After a mile I came to a vicarage,
Where the vicar's wife opened her door,
She sat me down in a comfortable chair,
And I was offered hot soup and coffee.
I watched her spectacled, snotty-nosed children
Sitting and playing their latest computer games.
I froze in horror when watching this lively screen,
Saw Wandil, whom I'd seen at Wandlebury,
That dragon spewing fire by those Saxon barrows,
Realised I'd seen the past in present and future.
I feared those demons ruled in areas of Britain,
Who sought control and dwelt in human hearts,
Herald the end time kingdom of Antichrist.
I went away from the Victorian vicarage,
Thinking of what I saw on the children's computer
Screen, that became for me the wide world soul;
And I sought to escape from this reality.
I was often tempted in the city, offered drugs,
But decided not to follow this downward path,
Night was approaching far too quickly,
Not realising my fortunes were about to change.
I was offered a bed in a night shelter,
Found my Emma working inside the kitchen.

Anglo-Saxon Saints and Heroes

This shows the divine power of saints who drove out the Saxon pagan gods and demonic oppression through spiritual warfare from the shrines and were able to bring about status and prosperity to the hamlets; also the heroes' continuous struggle with the Danes and Vikings.

In contrast a hermit takes a journey into the Anglo Saxon world, beginning from middle earth then on to Utgard, the land of the frost giants and dwarfs, descending into the dark underworld, climbing the bi-frost bridge into Asgard, and finally entering Valhalla.

Saint Ivo in Slepe

Ragged, rough and ready St Ivo,
Prophet, pilgrim, Persian Archbishop,
Whose soul and spirit soared and forged
Its fire and fuelled his fountain of faith.
He wended his way through wooded Houghton hill,
Through some ruins, aroused the Roman graveyard,
Spooked by its spirits and shadows that followed him
Down into a darkened dell, by a river
Slithering slowly, snaking through a meadow,
Where he met the might of middle earth;
He made his haunt here, in the hamlet of Slepe.
He sensed fear in those Saxons, that seared his heart,
Grovelling to their gods at the pagan shrines,
So sad to see their souls shackled in chains
Beneath the weird and wonderful world ash
That gleamed in green and gold in a blue sky.
He gazed at a rainbow that reached Asgard,
That ended up at the evil entrance of Valhalla.
Darkness descended that drained the depths of his soul,
Saw those Valkeries who veered in the vaults of heaven,
Sitting on their skeleton steeds snorting fire,
He was spellbound by their spears and shields flashing
In the lightning, that lit up like lashing whips.
He heard huntsmen and hounds howling in the welkin;
Woden in his broad-brimmed hat, blowing his horn,
Rode on Slepnier, who swung his shining hooves,
That thudded like thunder in throes of the thrashing dark
    storm.
                The saint was filled with fear,
                In all this darkness he'd borne,
                But he saw things like a seer,
                And a new day must dawn.

Evening fell, that looked like the forge's fire,
He met the brawny blacksmith beating on the anvil
With his hammer, harmonising with heaven above,
Its rhythm and rhyme rang the saint's prayers;
The saint picked up a powerful pair of tongs
And seized the Saxon sword red hot,
Buried its blade into a bubbling spring,
That sizzled and steamed. This sword of the Spirit,
Now tempered, its tip touched on eternity.
He heard a shepherdess sing his songs and strum her
   stringed lyre.
                    That touched the hamlet Slepe
                    With the saint's sacred fire
                    In Saxon souls so deep
                    And spread throughout the shire.

The saint saw showers of stars that fell from
Heaven, haunted him as he headed to lower earth,
Ghosts glared at him at the gateway of the fens;
He heard the hound of hell howling away,
That froze his feelings with fear in the mist;
He stood by the swamps steaming like cauldrons
That bubbled with bitterness in the black waters.
He watched a white witch whispering her rhymes,
Scorning the Saxons from her stony heart
And he smelt the sulphur smouldering in hell,
Chided by chilling chanting from the dead
And norms were whining from the wells of wyrd.
He saw the serpent Nidnogg surface in the fog,
Who groaned and gnawed at the ash's roots,
But he faced his foes and fiends in the fen so foul.

He'd seen them rise in hell
And the dead and demons growl,
That night the darkness fell,
He heard that giant wolf howl.

He roamed among those Roman ruins in Slepe,
Mosaics were mirrored on this moonlit night,
Sickened by its spirit that sallies and soars on high
Like an eagle, this evil empire spirit.
When he came to Cernunnos in his Celtic shrine,
This bearded god that blazed by the river,
He dozed and dreamed this dream of times past,
When bearded burly Britons, all blue with woad,
Danced before the burning Beltane fires
In a ritual that raged and reddened the skies,
Heightened when they heard the human sacrifice,
That screamed in terror at the top of its voice.
The Britons danced like devils until the dawn arose,
When the sun was streaming through the Stonehenge;
That golden circle glowed between the stones.
A dozen Druids were dancing and droning their lore,
Left their altar blood red,
Watching the ravens caw,
Feasted on one now dead,
Made their Celtic gods soar.

Saint Ivo's sword of the Spirit severed the darkness,
He'd wielded its words well deep in Saxon hearts,
Even the river ran in righteousness and peace
And the sacred springs sprung from eternity
That brought healing and happiness to the hamlet of
Slepe.

He sat by the shepherdess in the sunlit meadows,
Looking at the lambs, all leaping in joy,
He saw a lark soaring in the blue skies,
And sang songs with the shepherdess, who strummed her
    stringed lyre.
                That touched the hamlet Slepe
                With the saint's sacred fire
                In Saxon souls so deep
                And spread throughout the shire.

Saint Ivo's Spirit in Slepe

Peter was ploughing with his pair of oxen,
That stomped and snorted, steaming the autumn air,
The ritual of rooks that rose in those red skies
That followed him, feasting on fresh furrows
Of earth, on this eve of this eerie Halloween;
He plodded and plodded on, ploughing the field,
Felt that God had guided and goaded his will,
Now his ploughshare had struck a stone coffin.
He stopped and saw a sparkling silver chalice,
Lustre of coloured glass, glittering in the grave,
Some brooches belonging to this buried priest.
He was sore tempted to steal this sparkling find,
When he sensed the saint's fiery spirit
And fear forced him to flee to the bailiff.

Abbot Adnoth knelt before the altar in prayer,
There in Slepe's sacred Saxon church,
Where the brooches and bones blazed before God,
That brought crowds of the common folk to the cross;
He kept them pleading who this pious priest might be.
The thought of the people's purses pleased the Abbot,
Cheered to hear their coins clanging in his coffers.

A smithy, a simple soul, who learned God's will
Was drawn into a delightful dream that night;
When he saw the shining spirit of Saint Ivo,
His eyes were blinded by this blazing Archbishop;
He cringed at his crozier and the cross of Jesus
And shook when the saint's spirit spoke to him
To tell the bailiff about his buried brothers in Slepe.

The fear forced him to flee from his vision
And his room turned red with the saint's rage;
The smith asked the saint to give him a sign
And he felt such a blow from the bishop's crozier.
He awoke; his side was sore and searing in pain,
Ceased when he told the bailiff, who bellowed in
    unbelief,
He was chided for cherishing those old cobbler's bones.

Saint Ivo struck the sleeping Abbot that night
For churlishly comparing his bones to a cobbler's.
After he afflicted the ailing Abbot, that bailiff,
By chiding him and crippling him up with pain,
He had him ride his horse on the road to Ramsey Abbey
To tell about his brothers' bones buried in Slepe.

Two Abbots led this pious procession
Along the rough old Roman road
On that seven-mile stretch from Slepe to Ramsey;
Those brooding Benedictines in black-hooded cloaks
Carried the religious relics of Saint Ivo
And the blessed bones of his two brothers,
When a snowy white dove swooped down
Over those relics for the rest of the journey,
There in the wake of this weird and wonderful event.
Crowds of common folk cheered their arrival,
Some carrying Christ's cross and Christian gildings;
The people were dressed in purple and white,
With smoking censers and candelabra all ablaze,
In honour of their heavenly hero Saint Ivo,
That held such devotion so dear to their hearts.

The bells brought boundless blessings from heaven,
Holy angels sang from on high with the human choir.
The sun shone on those tanned shepherds watching
Their lambs light up and leap in joy
In the green meadows, all gilded in gold;
Birds whistled God's Word from the woods that day,
And the rolling rivers rang out in music,
The streams and springs sprung from eternity,
Now those relics were at rest in Ramsey Abbey.
Saint Ivo appeared to a prayerful, pious monk,
Spoke about setting a shrine before the altar.

February was gripped in freezing fog that evening,
That lingered and loomed so lazily around the Island,
Hoar frost had frozen the fields and trees.
The soaring Saxon abbey stood on the hillock,
Its clanging Vespers bell cut the cold crisp air,
But the Devil had dared to darken the abbey door.
Inside, the Benedictines in their black-hooded cloaks,
Their sandals squeaking on the cold stone floor,
Chanted the credo on this Candlemas night,
Swinging their smoking censers and scenting the air,
When Saint Ivo's shrine shone forth in light.
Some stricken monks suddenly straightened up,
Their bones cracked and clicked and were cured;
Some screamed and spewed out evil spirits
That went whining wryly out through the door.
The bondages were broken that bound them to Rome,
They'd snapped their chains and their spirits were set
    free;
It drove the devils and demons high in the air,
Until the floors of heaven flashed in fire,

Cherubim in their chariots chased after them
As far as that fiery furnace in hell.
The brothers all knelt before the saint in prayer,
Who'd dispelled the princes and powers of the air.

Abbot Adnoth argued that Saint Ivo's body
Be brought back to his burial ground in Slepe.
He had a monastery built in the middle of a croft,
With half his stone sepulchre set outside its wall,
Where holy waters heaved up in a healing spring,
That flowed forth so freely from his tomb.
Lepers were cleansed, the lame leaped in joy,
The blind could see, bondages broken from demons.

On August the ninth, in the afternoon, the Abbot
Brought back the brothers' bones in a silver casket,
He set them by the sacred sepulchre in the chapel;
That night saw golden pillars of light pierce the sky,
Shimmering for seven miles from Ramsey to Slepe,
He saw Saint Ivo and his saints on that starry road.
He joined the people pacing round the chapel
And his clergy carried crosses and smoking censers.
In the morning the meadows were gilded in gold,
So full of the freshness that fell from heaven;
On the blithe river that blazed in blessing,
He saw the springs that sprung from eternity,
From the saint who brought salvation to Slepe.

The Wanderer

Ragged old man, you roam through time,
Like fury, in a forest of fire that blackens,
Helps to harden your heart of flesh,
Drying your tongue, cracking your lips,
Lightens not the load that lies in your soul,
Neither shall the sun that sets in the west.

You watch that woeful waning moon,
Glowing, roving on the ripples of a lake,
Its shadows shimmering on a sheer cliff face;
You wait for wolves to wander from the forest
And hear them howling high on a slope,
You curse that comet streaming across the skies,
Make haste and hide in a hermit's cave,
Live in dread of death in this Dark Age.

Martyrdom of Saint Edmund

A blue shield bore three silver crowns,
King Edmund's emblem of the East Angles;
He trembled and talked before the throne of God,
With a love and longing, that lived in his heart.
He dreaded those Danes in their dragon ships,
Sailing in swirling seas to his Saxon coast;
He buried himself in bed, burdened by a nightmare,
Froze in fear at the fate of his kingdom.
He hearkened to that horn of the heathen Danes,
Saw his Saxons slain with sword and axe
And blood running, reddening the ruts of earth.
He trembled at torches thrown on thatched roofs,
That burned his buildings to black skeletons.
He watched wolves wending their way in the ashes,
Feasting on food from flesh of the dead,
Ravens and red kite soared right overhead.
He peered at the prophetess pouring out her rhymes
And spent some time staring at the stately oak;
Saw its bark had brightened to blood red,
Awoke all soaked in sweat at this omen.

He met the might of the Danes at Hoxne,
Hingwar and Hubba headed a huge army,
He bore the brunt of the battle so fierce;
Scared, he wandered like a sheep from his fold,
Despaired at the dead in ditches and fields,
Then he huddled under a humpbacked bridge.
He cursed the couple that caught sight of his golden
Spurs, that sparked on the stream in the moonlight.
He heard them hollering to those horrible Danes,
Who brought him to bear and bound him with ropes,
This hapless hero, hoisted up on the oak,

Oh, how he cursed this ordeal from Odin their god
And he'd live his life for the Lord Jesus Christ.
He faced the flying arrows that flew into his chest,
That bloodied his body to bright scarlet red.
When his limp and lifeless body was lowered down,
A swipe from a sword soon severed his head,
Thrown into a thicket of thorns in a wood;
His glorious face glowed more than his golden crown,
Where a white wolf waited and watched over him.
His spirit spoke to his Saxons on the search,
Thrice his voice was heard, "He's over here."

He was wheeled on a wagon to a Saxon church,
The saint stretched out on a slab of marble;
Holy water washed his wounds that healed,
A thread of purple pieced together;
Both his head and body became as one.
This saint was laid in a sacred shrine in the abbey,
But his spirit travelled through the troubled town,
Spotted that surly Sweyn Forkbread,
Furious his folk were forced to pay him tribute,
He destroyed the Dane, who died in pain,
From a spear that spiralled down from heaven.

A Saxon Soul

I, Harold the hermit, hated the heathen Danes
And saw those slayers of Saxon folk,
Like ghouls of greed, with their gold and silver,
I despised those demons of death in England,
Watched them wade in water to their ships,
Pulling on their oars, as one on open seas,
Dragon ships slithered through the surging waves.
After a while I went into a wide valley
And saw those scores of Saxons slain in war,
Raucous ravens rallied with red kite,
Pounced, picked and pecked at piles of the dead.
The hamlet's hall and houses all ablaze;
Flames flared in fury, like a funeral pyre,
Smoke belched and blackened the bowl of heaven.
At night I was eager to escape this evil,
Guided to glistening grass in a clearing,
Read some runes on the rocks in a circle,
That soaked my Saxon soul in magic.
Birches shone before those barrows on high,
Ferns on the forest floor all silvered
From the moon and mirrored her light.
I saw six elves near red toadstools,
Set in moss, so moist and mottled the rocks;
I wandered by waters, washing the stones,
There in the sand of a sacred spring that bubbled,
Burst into a fountain and filled the air.
Ash's roots ran beneath my feet,
I felt so fearful at their forces of power and
Wolves howling from the heart of the forest,
Further inflamed my fury that stirred,
My Saxon soul for supremacy in my kingdom,

Drove by demons of death through the gods,
Like the vile and violent Viking warriors,
Conquering with a cruel and cold spirit,
Echoed those eternal evils through the English

Eerie air,
Soon sent me fast asleep,
Close to a dragon's lair,
Where I heard his wings beat,
That stirred this dreadful nightmare.

Farther west I came to a wall at Utgard,
Leant on a ladder and laboured to the top,
Overwhelmed by this white wilderness,
Dicing with death through the driving snow,
Cold, crispy air chilling my bones,
Walking through this winter wonderland,
Found myself among those fiendish frost giants,
Shaking and shivering in stark terror.
I forged through a forest of fire and ice
To a place with a primordial palace like glass,
Where white, gloomy ghosts all glared at me,
Hollowed and haunted the hollow hallway.
I grappled on this glacier that cracked and growled,
Rumbling and rousing in rage and its age,
Yonder I saw where the Yggdrasil yielded its root,
That ran riot through this region of giants.
I was weathered and weary at the well of Mimir,
Drunk so deeply from its dark, still waters,
Surprised to see a stare from Woden's eye,
That made the mighty magic mountain glow.

Here I hit the heights of wisdom,
Saw a serpent surround a sunless sea,
Like a glowing giant girdle gripping the world,
With its bulging body and head, biting its tail,
I soaked up this sight in my spirit and
Marvelled as I moved down the misty mountain's

        High ridge,
      Where I reached my goal,
    Crossed straight over a bridge,
    Passed by a black witch troll,
    Right near an ancient village.

I came to a cave dripping with water,
Ash's roots ran riot on the ceiling,
Gleaming in gold, like a glittering night sky.
A ferryman forced me on this fiery lake,
It was Woden wearing his wide-brimmed hat,
Staring straight at me with his scarlet eye,
With a dark cape draping down his back,
A couple of crows cawed on his shoulders.
I found myself ferried to a faraway shore,
Goaded through those grinding gates of hell;
A howling hound haunted my soul,
Greeted by Garn, that gruesome guard dog,
Down in the deep domain of the dead;
Winching from whips wielded by demons,
I felt the fury from the underground
Rocky rivers running from a round cauldron,
Saw the slithering, small serpents hissing.

I was so near to Nidhogg in these nether regions,
Grieved at him gnawing and gorging at the ash's root,
I dreaded this demon of death in the depths

Of hell,
Among its furious flames,
Deep rumbling from the well,
Bound up in rattling chains,
Here in this prison cell.

After miles of misery, I came to middle earth,
Turned right and reached a rainbow bridge,
So tired and troubled on this trembling way,
Welcomed in the wondrous world of Asgard,
Here in a garden glowing in green and red gold
Burning in a background in the blue twilight,
Where I watched three white witches, the Norms,
Mouthing their magic of my moments through time,
Wailing over the waters in the Well of Wyrd;
All fraught with fear, I faced five hundred doors,
Gob-smacked, gripped with the grandeur of Valhalla.
I saw shimmering shields all soaring above,
Swords on the walls reflected in the firelight's glow.
I walked wearily up some worn stone steps,
Opened a door and was dazzled by daylight,
The sacred ash shot straight up in the heavens;
Its branches brightened in a brilliant blue sky,
A golden cock was crowing at the top.

I was so touched by the tall towers of the castle,
Cheered the chariots that carried the sun and moon,
Chased by wolves, wild as the winter wind
Blowing from the giant eagle's beating wings,
Fluttering so furious in foliage of the ash,
With four stags scoffing at its shivering leaves.
I heard the hounds howling all around,
My Saxon soul soared in a storm of darkness,
As Thor hurled his hammer with such a force;
It thudded and thundered through the thin air,
Flashed and flared in the floors of heaven.
I watched Woden in the welkin, winding his horn,
Riding his stallion Sleipnir, swinging his hooves,
Headed by his hounds, that howled and snarled;
I saw them sniffing and smelling for blood,
Breathing brimstone and bile from their jaws;
I saw the scrawny steeds' steaming nostrils,
Ridden by rough and ruddy huntsmen,
That haunted the hamlets, halls and shires.
I moved over mountains and moonlit meadows

In flower,
Admired those silver streams
In this late midnight hour,
Where I woke from my dreams,
My soul all filled with power.

Viking Voyage to Hell

Three Viking ships bobbed up and down,
High in the North Sea's great swell,
An ill wind drove these beasts along,
That came out from the jaws of hell.

The heathens dragged their ships on shore,
Armed to the teeth with sword and axe,
When they sounded their battle horn,
Knew Saxon hearts would melt like wax.

First they preyed upon the abbey,
Like greedy hogs so brash and bold,
Soon would pounce on innocent lambs,
Like ravenous wolves inside a fold.

Those pagans paused and listened to
The monks' low voices at Lindisfarne
Singing holy plainchant at Vespers,
Verses from the twenty third psalm.

When they broke in through the door,
Dashed in quick as a flash flood,
Wielded their weapons of war in fury,
The grey stone floor ran with blood.

Archangel came down from heaven,
Made the golden cross blaze in light,
Almost blinded the grovelling warriors,
All caught up in this pitiful sight.

The Vikings torched the ancient abbey,
Devil laughed in the fiery glow,
Cursed them with his demonic voice,
They'd journey into his raging inferno.

They roamed on a never-ending sea,
Were driven by the dragon's breath,
Clutched the gold with skeleton fingers,
Fatigue had starved them all to death.

The fleet of ships sailed through the mist,
Zombies groaning there on board,
Odin's eye glowed red as the sun,
Now lit the fiord like a forge.

Norse gods whined in the heights of Asgard,
Soon filled the air with awe,
Lightning flashed on rows of shields
And treasure from the spoils of war.

Bitter north wind flapped the sails
Behind each dragon's rampant head,
The long ships left their glistening wake,
Right near the island of the dead.

A sword came from a dragon's mouth,
Enhanced and touched its deep desire,
Spurred on the burning warrior spirit,
That spewed its streams of living fire.

The howling wolves on mountainside,
Witch trolls shook an ancient bridge,
Roused the giants in forest glades,
There in the land beyond the ridge.

This Viking voyage all filled with dread,
The splashing oars downward beat,
Its dripping blades disturbed the waters
And a serpent sprung from the deep.

Odin's couple of ravens appeared,
Prompted whom he should devour,
Squawking around there to and fro,
That whipped up dark demonic power.

Scrawny eagle screeches above,
With talons trained upon its prey,
On murdered monks in ghostly form,
Like wraiths in mist all black and grey.

A grim smile came from every skull,
Their souls enslaved and shackled in chains,
Death now reigned inside the hull,
Doomed ships spiralled down in flames.

Sutton Hoo

Evening skies burned in red and gold,
When those pagan winds still blew,
At the burial of King Raedwald,
There in a barrow at Sutton Hoo.
Woden stood in his broad-brimmed hat,
Stroking his beard and twitching his eye;
His pair of ravens sat on his shoulders,
Flapped their wings and flew in the sky.
He joined the lost in a heathen song,
Sorrow came from those Saxon lips,
They gathered round the grave in a throng,
Looking down on their sunken ship;
The deck shone in red, blue and gold,
All that treasure of King Raedwald.

The Shepherdess

A shepherdess sits upon a rock,
She pitches her glorious singing voice,
Her fingers pluck her tuneful lyre,
That make the mountains and hills rejoice.

Down in a valley she clasps her crook,
Watches those sheep under her care,
Paddles her feet in a rocky stream,
She breathes in fresh, cool mountain air.

She gazes into a pure blue sky,
There at those mountain peaks of snow,
And those rugged mountaintops
Mirror in the lake so clear below.

At evening she plays her harp again,
Beneath the eagles' wings that soar,
Her high voice echoes through the valley,
Where rushing streams and waterfalls roar.

Etheldreda's Dream

Etheldreda found her path,
Held onto her pilgrim's staff,
Dressed in a mantle of emerald green,
Once was crowned a Saxon queen;
Her golden braids hung from her veil,
Brushed her cheeks that looked so pale,
A peace lit up her gentle face,
Her bright blue eyes shone forth in grace.
She came to where some roses grew,
That glowed beneath the heavenly blue.
She loved the roses' deep blood red,
Thought of when her Saviour bled,
Stayed in this rose garden she'd found,
Then she pushed her staff in the ground.

There she slept by a bubbling stream;
After a while she started to dream:
Her pilgrim's staff had taken root,
From which green leaves began to shoot
And spread its branches into the sky.
Here she saw two black ravens fly
Through a window at Valhalla's hall.
Sharp spears lined the chamber's wall;
Above, nine hundred shields all gleamed;
On ghostly Saxon king and queen,
The warrior swords reflected fire,
Stirred and sparked her deepest desire;
Woden was seated with Frey and Thor,
Teased her about the necklace she wore.

When she woke from her ordeal,
Having spun on fortune's wheel,
Found her staff came out in bloom,
That night she slept beneath the moon;
Why she faced this demonic trial,
Later became abbess in Ely's Isle.

The Slaying of Fenrir

A shepherd drives his sheep along,
Near where a weaving river flows,
He watches maidens laugh and splash,
Here in the heart of summer's glow.
Farther down this winding river,
He leaves his sheep to graze on a slope,
Then looks for shelter from the sun
And he shades beneath an oak.

His flock of sheep is safe in the field,
Under moon and stars at night;
Beds down with his pair of sheepdogs
Beside a fire that's burning so bright.
He sees a comet stream across the skies
And he fears it's a sign of fate,
When passing over the Saxon hamlet,
There on the other side of the lake.

Around midnight he wakes from his sleep,
That brings a stirring in his soul;
He sees that wicked, giant grey wolf
Swallow some of his sheep whole.
He dreads this creature that roams the earth,
Faces up to this fiend most foul,
He freezes at its demonic presence,
Watches him lift his head and howl.

He stares inside the wolf's nostrils
And he sees those fires in hell,
Finds he's choked from its steaming breath,
How he hates that brimstone smell,

The glare from its glowing yellow eyes,
His bristling coat all silvery grey,
That moment he bares his jagged teeth,
Worried he'd finish up as prey.

Now he's filled with terror and steps
Back from the swipe of its curving claws;
He makes a sudden dart for his spear,
Dodges its open dripping jaws
And he moves in for the kill,
Hopes his weapon will find its mark,
Robs that wolf of his wicked will
And he thrusts his spear in his heart.

The Harrowing of Hell

A pair of horses dragged a harrow,
It broke up furrows with its spikes,
Raked bones from a Saxon barrow,
Somewhere near the Devil's Dyke.
Fluffy clouds all tinted purple,
Among those skies turned dark red.
Rooks and crows flew in a circle,
Mocked this harrowing of the dead;
Those lost in hell began to scream
In this Christian season of Lent,
Where suffering souls cried, "Redeem!"
Pleaded with Him who was sent.
This caused the pair of horses to shy,
They rode over the burning dead,
For none of their sins would ever die,
They'd not believed on him who bled.

Hereward the Wake

The ancient Anglo Saxon abbey stood
High on a hill where Hereward the Wake
Mingled with the medieval monks at Candlemas,
He sang their sonorous sacred plainchant,
Worshipped in words of wisdom from the psalms,
Bowed before the beautiful Marian shrine
That glittered in gold and glorious precious stones.
He received the bread, the broken body of Christ,
Sipped wine from the shining silver chalice,
Deep in prayer and perfect peace from his Saviour
In the heights of holiness from the Holy Spirit
Descending like a dove from the dome of heaven;
He saw the presence, power and purity of angels,
All burned so brightly before the Almighty God.

Although revenge had ravaged and ruled his heart,
So stunned and sickened by the sadistic Normans,
His brother's blood burned in his brain so grieved
To see his head stuck on a spear at his gate.
The Wake led his warriors of war through
The misty marshes to Medhamstede Abbey.
He battled and barraged, unable to breach the walls;
This rebel raged and roused dark terror,
When blazing branches burned the Bolhithe Gate;
This Saxon soon seized and sacked the abbey,
Took his torches to town and razed it to the ground.

He waited and waylaid William's army,
Who crossed with care on the causeway at Aldreth;
He was wary of his witch in a wooden tower,
Heaping her handfuls of hateful curses upon him;

He fired those reeds, that raged so red and crackled
With wrath in the wind and wrecked his enemies,
Bellowing on the blazing bridges as they sank
In the bogs that bubbled like a steaming cauldron.
He was dazzled by demons darting in the flames,
Waved their wicked black wings, those fiends;
Their hideous horns came from the halls of hell,
That seemed to spur his spirit of death.
He swung his sword and slew the last of them,
As he watched the witch wobbling in her burning tower,
Screaming in the smoke and fire in horror,
And she fell into that fiery inferno.

One night he slept so smug and soundly in his bed,
And knights broke into his bedroom like a bull;
He woke and went so white with rage,
And he seized his shield and sword, Brainbiter.
He floored fifteen fellows with his great strength,
And brandished the bloody blade of his sword;
Fell when a shower of spears stuck in his back,
Hurled by the knights; he knelt on his knees in pain,
Slung his shield, that spun and struck a man dead,
Then fell face down on the floor and died.

Fantasies of a Dairymaid

A dairymaid of Viking descent
Lived in the small village of Dent,
Never a fairer maiden you'd meet,
Often walked that cobbled street,
Swished around in her long, red skirt
And she looked so alive and alert.
She loved to hear the skylark's trill,
When tripping by a rushing rill.
A breeze ruffled her ginger hair,
That flowed so freely in the air;
When she came to the dairy farm,
She thrilled the folk with all her charm.

She strolled back home through misty fells,
Found where her Viking spirit dwells,
There in the evening's dark red glow,
Thought of times so long ago.
First she heard some beating oars,
Saw their ships on Saxon shores.
This feeling of war gave her a thrill,
Followed the warriors down the hill.
Then she heard their battle horn,
The hamlet ravaged like a storm;
She watched them wielding sword and axe,
Saw the Saxons' hearts melt like wax,
All the buildings blazed with fire,
Found this heightened her heathen desire.
She waved to Valkyries in the sky,
All lit from Odin's glowing eye.

Ethelfleda

My father's words welled up within my soul
And I must go to Mercia and marry Earl Athelred.
I was sixteen and sobbed in sorrow all that day,
As I wended my way to a Wessex church,
There on my knees before the King of heaven.
I saw the light of the Lord, like a lamp burning;
It showed me the state of the Saxon churches,
How Mercia had met the might of those heathen Danes.

I loved being that lady leading the Mercians,
There on my silver steed in the Severn valley;
I wore my shining suit of Saxon armour
And my fair hair flowed from my battle helmet;
I held my blue and silver shield of Mercia,
All ready to fight with my freshly forged sword.
I watched the weapons of war glinting
There in the hands of my hundreds of Saxon horsemen.

How my heart heaved at the horrors before me!
Saw flames of fire that filled the Severn valley,
Buildings burned and blazed in the hamlet.
I saw a red demon revel and rage in the flames;
Who'd been freed from that fiery furnace of hell.
Crows were cawing and circling in the skies.
I heard Saxon souls screaming from their blood,
Saw Valkyries who veered into that valley of fire.
I sobbed at the sight of Saxons killed
By those Danes, who raided and ravaged our land.

Like a wolf I waited and watched from the slope
At the Danes, how they drifted in droves below,
My riders and I rode in rage in their midst;
I fought like fury with my fiery sword,
And I wrought many wounds on my warrior foe;
My sword had slain scores of them,
For God's strength surged through my body.
Death came to those Danes; I drove them from our land.
Christians were chanting in the churches to God,
Angels sung in Saxon in the Severn valley.

The Dragon Slayer

Years ago a Saxon warrior
Armed with shield and glowing sword
Went to fight a fiery dragon,
Found him crouched at Meadow Ford.

At noon he faced that angry creature,
Wondered if he'd be forced to yield
When it breathed its flames of fire,
But holy water drenched his shield.

Its whipping tail whizzed past his head;
Stepped aside from its curving claws,
Rolled his body out of the way,
There from the snap of its evil jaws.

He summoned his last reserves of strength,
Thrust his sword in its scaly hide;
His blade was buried to its hilt,
Smoke poured out its wounded side.

When it rose and flapped its wings,
He blocked his ears at the deafening roar,
Then it flew so high in the heavens;
This victory made his spirit soar.

He saw the fiend in forked lightning
Fall to earth with such a thud,
When it started to pour with rain,
Stood there soaked in all its blood.

Woden and the Ash

A red fire flickered inside a cave,
Bearded dwarfs worked round a forge,
Hammered Woden's spear on the anvil,
That echoed through a narrow gorge.

After their spear had glowed white hot,
They gripped it with their pair of tongs,
Watched it sizzling in a magic spring,
They bellowed out Old Saxon songs.

Then they saw a blazing comet
Reflect upon a moonlit lake,
They knew those foreboding nine days,
And were the seal for Woden's fate.

How they shook when the thunder crashed,
Woden's body pierced with their spear,
They watched him hanging on the ash,
Made them hug together in fear.

They stood before the glowing runes,
Listened to its words being read,
Saw the extent of Woden's power,
Shocked he came back from the dead.

A Visit to Valhalla

I boarded my whaling vessel that grim Friday,
My sailors checked the rigging, ropes and sails,
After a while I watched my anchor weighed.

I sailed the ocean for days in search of whales,
There with my crew on my ship, the Rose Marie,
Who did their daily tasks with tooth and nail.

In those buffeting billows of the sea,
I heard a seaman shout from the crow's nest,
About black, angry clouds that enshrouded me.

Later on I embraced that howling tempest;
In wind and wave, my ship danced like a reel,
For hours and hours my crew were given no rest.

I helped my helmsman wrestle with the wheel,
Saw a sailor fall from the dripping mast,
And I heard some rats squeal from the keel.

How I cursed the strength of this stormy blast;
My ship spun in the wildest of whirlpools,
And I hit the deck and laid there aghast.

Raving demons glared at me like ghouls
As I spiralled into the bowels of the earth,
In this tempest that defied all nature's rules.

I awoke on deck, all soaked in salt and surf,
Where scarlet flames lit up a sunless sea;
Above I saw some gold that filled me with mirth,

Among the spreading roots of a giant ash tree,
That was hanging inside this dripping cave;
I wondered where this ancient place could be.

For here I felt neither wind nor wave,
What force of evil drove my ship along?
It looked as though my crew had got the plague.

I saw some ghostly monks appear in a throng,
Their skulls in drooping black hoods, smiling in evil,
Started to sing in strange plainchant and song.

In this cave that looked like a cathedral,
I listened to the monks' eerie voices echo,
Which drew my being into their dark ritual.

How this power soon made my spirit glow;
It lifted up my soul in this pagan shrine,
It reached those heights of idolatry below.

I found myself caught up in eternal time,
Watched Thor hurling his thunderbolt of fire
Upon some Saxon ships; I counted nine.

I saw those wrecks all burn like a funeral pyre,
Grieved at the Saxon seamen screaming in pain,
Cursed my fate and fortune that seemed so dire,

It seemed my voyage had all been in vain,
Ended up in a place where demons dwell,
This living nightmare proved to be a bane,

When I saw that fiend unchained from hell
Made those waters bubble like witches' cauldrons,
And several of my sailors gave a yell.

I saw this creature shoot up fifty fathoms,
Heard this slithering serpent Midgard roar,
That fared worse than the fiercest of dragons.

It grabbed my sailor between his massive jaws,
Then I shot a harpoon spear in its throat;
He writhed and sunk down to the dark sea floor.

Water swamped my ship, but kept afloat;
It soon steadied on the light's return,
But surprised to find it drifted into a moat,

And I felt I was being dragged astern,
Jumped on land with my crew beneath a wall,
The moat caught fire and saw my old ship burn.

My heart was broken and felt as bitter as gall,
My lantern cast shadows on the spiral grey steps,
Overcome by the sheer mystery of it all.

I found that I'd broken out in a cold sweat,
When I heard some rattling chains in a dungeon,
That place where legions of evil demons were kept.

I saw a fiery devil chase one of my men,
Froze when death had seized him there on the run;
Cobwebs covered his skeleton, there and then.

I saw some glowing coals as red as the sun,
Right where Woden's sword was being forged,
By the dwarfs who spoke in a Saxon tongue.

I watched the white hot blade light up the gorge;
It was tempered where magic springs abound,
That fired up the ugly dwarfs even more.

Then I seized the sword and swung it around;
Its magical powers soon filled me full of hope,
But doubted when I faced a ghostly hound,

And I ran, slid straight down a slippery slope.
I came face to face with a waiting ferryman,
There in his drooping black-hooded cloak,

His bony finger pointed me where to stand
And I felt the sluggish ferry veer
Between the icy palaces, that looked so grand.

I saw some ghostly bearded giants all rear
Their ugly heads and breathe all over me,
Then saw some fiery stones suddenly appear

That once had covered the earth in all its glory,
Before the fall of Satan and his kind;
I saw his kingdom glittering beneath the sea.

The ferryman left me and my crew behind,
Upon the shore I came to some steps like before,
Went straight up and wondered what else I'd find.

After a while I opened a creaking door
And saw some festive tables in a massive hall,
Set with horns of mead and roasted wild boar.

My spirit captured the sheer grandeur of it all;
I gazed into the ceiling of gleaming shields
And thousands of spears that lined every wall.

Now I'm driven by fate and fortune's wheels,
When warriors came and tucked into their feast;
These heroes, who died on the English battlefields,

All served by Valkyries, those fair-haired beasts,
I couldn't believe I'd see these ancient foes
Wield their weapons and thought my life would cease,

Then I faced up to Woden's Saxon heroes;
I fought, yet felt like a man already dead,
Wondering if I'd escape from death's throes.

My magic sword half blinded them as I fled
Straight up some steps, with my crew behind me;
At last I reached the top of a tower in dread

And saw a clear blue sky that filled me with glee,
Found my spirit soared like an eagle on high;
Then it landed on top of a giant ash tree.

At last a way of escape had caught my eye;
I jumped in the ash's branches and climbed down,
Sighed and no longer thought my end was nigh.

I was glad my aching feet had touched the ground
And I ran in the forest before night fell,
When I heard Woden's hunting hounds

And feared his heroes joined the hunt as well;
I saw their horses breathing fire and brimstone
Into the skies, light up the forest and dell.

All out of puff, I ached in every bone,
When a hermit beckoned me to his cave
And I waited until my hunters went home.

What relief I felt when the holy man prayed,
And I was so thankful to see the next morning;
What a soothing song those thrushes made!

Then I heard a beautiful shepherdess singing;
Her soaring voice sweetened the morning air,
Like a skylark trilling high on the wing.

How the sun sparkled upon her hair
That ran down her gown in golden tresses!
I'd never seen a maiden look so fair.

I saw her lily white flesh as she undressed,
Then she bathed in the waters of a stream;
Found myself gazing upon her breast.

Among the shepherd girls she's my queen,
Led her sheep so safely, with guiding hand;
Her white lambs spread all over the hills so green.

I came to a hamlet set in Saxon England,
The sun had reddened the thatched roofs at evening,
I watched the woe that weighed on every man.

Inside a hall I heard some women wailing,
Then saw a pair of oxen pulling a wagon;
Mourners followed their dead Saxon King.

I heard fierce wolves howling, roused from their den,
But watchful shepherds' fires were burning bright,
And high above the moon I saw an omen,

And I watched a blazing comet's tail of light,
That lit the silver birches around those barrows;
Ghosts of kings and queens appeared that night.

I felt these signs increased the mourners' woes,
Lifted the king's body from the wain,
There on a funeral pyre, where fierce flames rose.

After a while I went from where I came
Through the forests and ferns, and saw a lake,
And I met that shepherdess again.

I froze as her face began to change in shape,
Found this woman, who made me feel so glad,
Had turned to a werewolf, so full of hate!

The whole of my being shook, I felt so scared,
When it laid its head back and gave a howl;
Its yellow eyes blazed, with its teeth all bared.

I never thought I'd face a fiend so foul,
And I managed to dodge its crooked claws,
Somehow I'd stop it going on the prowl.

I stood in awe of its teeth and dripping jaws,
My magic sword soon took it by surprise;
Wounded, it went into the wood on all fours.

I fell asleep and woke to the dawn's red skies,
Came to a valley and saw a Saxon abbey,
Looked and I could hardly believe my eyes

When I saw the Viking ships on the sea
And heathens stepped upon the Saxon shores;
How I shuddered at the size of this army.

My heart sank as I watched the warriors of war
Sack a Saxon abbey, that burned in flames;
Heathens came rushing out of the abbey door.

I knew the Vikings would go as quick as they came,
Carried their gold and silver down to their ships;
All so pleased about their ill-gotten gains.

When I turned I met my men and the hermit,
Watched the gates of heaven open wide,
There to receive the murdered brothers' spirits,

And saw the angels' trumpets that gleamed inside,
I heard a thousand angelic choirs all sing,
When those martyred monks were glorified.

I knew those saints had met their heavenly King,
Fields and forests glowed in golden light;
Crystal lakes and streams sparkled in blessing.

When the heavens closed, it went black as night,
I heard the sound of Woden's hunting horn;
His heroes and black hounds proved an awful sight.

I'd never seen such fury released in a storm:
Valkyries' fiery spears were glowing red,
Chasing my weary crew like a frightened fawn.

Saxons' skeleton horses filled me with dread,
While their riders wielded their weapons of war,
That filled me full of terror, as I fled.

I boarded Woden's ship that lay on the shore,
Found myself trapped inside a rocky bay,
Upon the waves that gave a mighty roar.

I felt the hunters were seeking me as prey,
Sparks were flying from my shield and sword;
I thought my crew and I would die today.

A giant-sized billow swept me overboard,
I struggled in the water and thought I'd die,
And I placed my life in the hands of the Lord.

A thousand years had passed before my eyes,
The sea had washed my crew and me on sand
Upon the shore, beneath the sun-filled skies.
I was so glad to escape from Saxon England.

Dark Celtic Past

This section paints a picture of the pagan rituals in ancient Britain, such as those practised throughout history in Wales and parts of Cornwall, and describes the spiritual atmosphere created by idolatry.

Celtic Cornwall

One day I walked in Gogmagog's
Footsteps along the Cornish cliffs
And stared at rugged rocks, that rose
From the sea, all in a line,
Like a humpbacked giant sea serpent,
That waited there, ready to strike.
I faced a fierce knight frozen in time,
Standing among those castle rocks,
There at the tip of Land's End.
Down in a cove I heard ghostly
Sailors screaming in crashing waves,
That never-ending, haunting ship's
Bell, that took me back in time.

Beyond grey granite rocks I roved
Into a secret fairy garden,
Greeted by fairies with golden wings,
That hovered over the glorious sea-pinks.
I stood among some Hottentot figs,
Blazing so bright in yellow and purple;
Elves in green popped up between,
Who led me into their elfin fair,
Set in a picturesque background of
Golden sands and turquoise sea,
I watched its wavelets lapping the shore.

Among the swirling inland fog,
I came to a circle of Celtic stones,
Beating there in psychic energy,
That riveted those ravens to the rocks.

Darkness fell, I saw ghostly
Faces grinning, all blue with woad,
Heard their tongues that spoke of war;
I felt such power from the Druid Queen,
Dazzled by her purple gown,
Golden torc and Celtic crown
Silvered by the mellow moon,
That filled my soul with cosmic power.

There in the throes of morning sunrise,
I turned and faced the ancient Green Man,
Clothed in ivy from head to toe,
Holding a blazing torch in his hand;
I was trapped in this Celtic ritual,
Until I felt at one with nature,
And danced among the Celtic warriors,
Before a score of Druid priests,
Heard them chanting cosmic rhythms,
There in that circle of standing stones.
I became part of this living legend,
Saw Belenos – red-faced, bearded sun –
Manifest all his power through nature,
Which changed those leaves that shone like gold.
I heard some Celtic music that flowed
From rushing streams and bubbling springs,
Met with Ludd, all dripping wet.
I faced an ancient stag that bowed
His antlers and drank from the magic waters.

Next morning I stared at the Cornish landscape,
Haunted by those cloudy skies,
Pierced with spears from the golden sun,
Opened the hall of those Celtic gods.
I stood there gripped, lost in a maze,
When I caught a glimpse of Belenos,
Stunned by his face of bearded flame,
I watched him move through shifting clouds,
Over a dark grey, haunting sea,
Here in ancient Celtic Cornwall.

Bodmin Moor

Gathering ravens circle and caw,
A dragon's wings beat in the air,
Now darkness falls on Bodmin Moor.

That dragon crouches high on a tor,
Breathes his fire and lands in his lair.
Gathering ravens circle and caw,

Anger the dragon, who gives a roar,
Over the blood-stained altar there,
Now darkness falls on Bodmin Moor.

Some Druids' souls begin to soar,
Almost seems more than they could bear;
Gathering ravens circle and caw,

While Druids chant their ancient lore,
By those Beltane fires that flare,
Now darkness falls on Bodmin Moor.

The Druids' ritual, demons' war,
Forked lightning strikes everywhere,
Gathering ravens circle and caw,
Now darkness falls on Bodmin Moor.

Mystery of Valle Crucis

At evening a merlin's wings hovered,
There in the mountains green and grey;
It swooped in a valley with talons trained,
Until its claws had gripped its prey.

Druids played heed to this omen,
They made a sacrifice in blood
That called up nature's river god,
Found they evoked the power of Ludd.

A pool reflected the abbey so clear,
Now bubbled like a witch's cauldron,
Reflecting frenzied Celtic souls,
There in the town of Llangollen.

That following night the Druid priests
Spoke with voice of an ancient bard,
Over those crackling Beltane fires,
Made the mountain air all marred.

Lightning flashed and lit the abbey,
High winds whistled deep from its well,
Magic summoned by Druid priests,
And fires of fury roared from hell.

Demon horsemen looked down on the abbey,
Prepare for spiritual warfare,
Rode like thunder into the valley,
They were halted by Cistercians' prayer.

After the monks had broken their fast,
Praised their God who'd set them free,
Blessings blew through the Horseshoe Pass,
That touched the winding River Dee.

Fairy Glen

See the golden sunlight falls,
Leafy boughs on cavern walls,
Deeper, emerald shades of green,
River flashes, rocks between,
Hark, those thundering waters roar,
Make those fairy spirits soar,
Over the clinging moss and lichen,
Light that rugged Fairy Glen.

Evening sun begins to tire,
Blazes like a forge's fire,
Makes the canyon shine all red,
And water in that riverbed
Hammers on the rock and stone,
Making music of its own,
Rouses a dragon from its den,
Flaps its wings round Fairy Glen.

Under the silver moonlight's glow,
Raging torrent there below
Finds its rest in stagnant pool,
Where those fairy spirits rule;
Showers of golden fireflies spark,
Show up elves there in the dark;
Waters bubble like a cauldron,
Haunt that eerie Fairy Glen.

See the golden sunlight falls,
Leafy boughs on cavern walls,
Deeper, emerald shades of green,
River flashes, rocks between,

Hark, those thundering waters roar,
Make those fairy spirits soar,
Over the clinging moss and lichen,
Light that rugged Fairy Glen.

A Witch at Beltane

One dark and windy night a wicked Welsh witch
Landed with her besom broom, smooth as the breeze.
At the mouth of the Aber Falls, she put out her
Silvery tongue, which licked the rocky cauldron below.
She stared straight down the river with her evil eyes
At the surging waters, swollen by the winter rains.
She stretched out her skeleton fingers and cast a spell;
Luminous fairies and elves danced on the rocks,
That made her spirit move along in the river's motion,
Spewing in torrents and beating the rocks like a hammer,
Seething, foaming and lisping among the rocky pools.
She woke the ancient Celtic sleeping river gods,
That she heard groaning from the deep, dark caverns.
She stepped shivering out of that cold, raging river;
Black rags clung to her bones, all dripping with water.
With her glowing red eyes set back deep in her skull,
She found her hard, black heart was beating in anger
And she crept like a shadow through that Welsh village.
She stopped and stared inside a tavern's window
At Marion Jones strumming the strings of her harp,
Who mourned the dreadful death of her demon lover.
The witch cursed Marion from her unhallowed grave
Who came up fuming from the fiery plains in hell;
To take revenge that day she blazed in the bonfire's
    flames
Before Marion and the village, who stood there laughing.
The witch chuckled when the Druids in the tavern
Took young Marion up to Dragons Green Hill;
She saw her forced in a wicker basket woven with
    flowers,
Then set ablaze over the rocky, raging river;
Water met with fire on this wild Beltane night.

Belenos at Beltane

Belenos – red-faced, bearded sun –
You fuel the Britons' souls' desire,
Watch them dance with frenzied feet,
Then make their passions burn like fire.

You shine so bright on meadows green
And help the morning songbirds sing,
All nature feels your warm embrace,
That sparkles in your bubbling spring.

Now you light red eventide,
Stir wheeling rooks above the trees,
See ravens peck a black bull's carcass,
Rouse Beltane blood upon the breeze.

Among the twinkling stars at night,
You silver the moon's last quarter,
glowing over river, stream,
Your natural spring all weaving water.

Belenos – red-faced, bearded sun –
You fuel the Britons' souls' desire,
Watch them dance with frenzied feet,
Then make their passions burn like fire.

Sun Sacrifice

Celtic red-faced, bearded sun,
Time for sacrifice has come,
All in tune with every spook,
Demons dance with cloven hoof.

See those ritual rooks encircle
Under skies all red and purple,
Time for witches' souls to soar,
Open up dark nature's door.

The Green Man stands there all aglow,
Clothed in leaves from head to toe,
How his blazing torches inspire,
Set those witches' hearts on fire.

Spirits stir the old hags' dance,
Deepest solar powers enhance;
Feel the pulse from Mother Earth,
Praise its joys of bright new birth.

After sun wakes from its bed,
Blood will stain the altar red;
Virgin screams in ritual death
Bring new life to nature's breath.

The Green Man

The Green Man bares his torch's flame,
Lights those depths of the human soul,
That brings forth bright spring days again
And leafy boughs play out his role.

His spirit hides beneath the bark,
Straight down the roots to a land of fear;
Ancient giants tread round in the dark,
Demonic Celtic spirits appear.

Way in the forest evergreen,
He stands beside some bubbling springs,
Hears those ancient Druids chant,
Who worship all created things.

There in future, present and past,
He makes his presence felt through time,
Hides his face behind a mask,
Always there in the human mind.

Queen Boadicea

Boadicea rides in her war chariot,
Stares at the hovering high hawk,
She's dressed in a blue and scarlet gown,
There in her crown and golden torcs.

When she meets her Celtic warriors,
This tortured queen of the Iceni tribe
Joins forces with the Trinovantes,
She leads them forth in power and pride.

The queen stands inside her chariot,
Ginger hair flows down her waist,
Cracking her whip over her horses,
That gallop at a deadly pace.

She drives along those Roman roads,
Knives are flashing on her wheels;
It makes the ground rumble like thunder,
Matches the anger she deeply feels.

Later she ravages those Roman towns,
Moves around like lightning flashes,
She leaves their buildings roaring in flames,
That turn to a heap of grey ashes.

After the battle she visits the Druids;
There in those shadows at wooden henge
She feels the power of her Celtic gods
Create new fire in her revenge.

She glares at the small Roman army
Advancing in rank, who lock their shields;
She freezes before their showers of javelins,
Sees her men cut down in the fields.

Her chariots are blocked by all her dead,
She's thrown in chaos and faces defeat,
Her tribes tremble in their wagons,
Block and bar her way of retreat.

Now her army lies there slaughtered,
She's filled with enmity and strife,
Pours poison in her chalice of wine,
Drinks the potion and ends her life.

Druids and Stonehenge

Druids gathered round Stonehenge,
Waited for their gods to appear,
Droning in their hooded white cloaks,
That brought about a realm of fear.

They laid a virgin on the altar,
Watched the raised sharp ritual knife,
There all ready to pierce her heart,
Thought her death would bring forth life.

How they loved the summer solstice,
Red-circled sun between the stones,
Found it evoked a deity
Dry as a dead man's brittle bones.

When they whispered words on the plain,
Those cosmic winds began to blow,
Aroused the curse of eternal death,
There in the sky's dark scarlet glow.

A brilliant light dazzled the priests,
Which brought about an awesome silence,
They heard those thundering horses' hooves,
That shook the bright green earth in violence.

They saw the demons appear on horseback,
The climax of this religious rite,
They spotted them in those standing stones,
Spellbound from their blazing light.

Winter Solstice

He hears grey wolves howling there
   under a forest full moon,
Enhanced by the roar from the raging wild rapids below,
He speaks his enchantments
   and meets with the Celtic chief god,
That antlered Green Man
   who is covered in leaves all aglow,

This Druid in hooded white cloak in this winter solstice.
His golden sharp sickle cuts mistletoe from the oak.
He stares at its white coloured berries
   that glow like a pearl;
Now puts them so carefully into a sacred white cloak.

He joins other Druids all chanting
   in Celtic strange tongues;
He's standing before the white bulls' pairs of horns
   being bound,
Then spreads out his hands to black ravens
   in the rising red morn,
Just like the bulls' blood
   that is soaking the sacred ground.

The fiendish priest leads a young girl
   in a forest green grove,
To lie on an altar to face that sharp sacrificial knife,
Now pierces her heart as he watches her blood
   soak the altar;
It touches those dark powers of nature
   that spring into life.

Then started to prophecy war
    to those British proud Chieftains,
In scarlet and purple long gowns
    and in golden bright torcs,
He stirs up the warriors
    wearing blue woad and black masks,
It moves their young spirits now
    soaring above the high hawk.

He watches the screaming huge wicker man
    burn on the hill,
That bursts into crackling fierce flames
    like a funeral pyre,
Then joins in the tribal wild dance by a watery rill,
He's moved by the rising sun's wheel
    in the dawn's red fire.

He hears the dark thunder god, Tarnis,
    thud high in heaven,
While bearded sun Belenos blazes in horse-drawn chariot.
He sees how it shimmers in streams
    and on bubbling springs,
Like sparkling spearheads on the lake
    that light up his spirit.

A Pilgrimage Through Ireland

A pilgrim watched a cliff-high hawk
Beneath the shining tears of the sun,
Sparkling on the fresh green valley;
Its lake bubbled like a cauldron,
It churned up those years of yesterday,
That dimmed his path on Pilgrims' Way.

Late afternoon, he rested his head
On half-hidden stone of destiny,
Tossed and turned in nature's bed
Under the branches of a tree;
When its young leaves all unfurled,
It whisked him into the Celtic world.

During his slumber, the grey rock screamed
When those spirits started to rave,
Seemed to enhance his troubled dream;
He stood before dark Queen Marve,
Arrayed in blue and purple gown,
And he was dazzled by her crown.

It seemed hours before he awoke,
Early on that summer morn;
He came across some fairy folk,
Watched them tease a leprechaun;
How this creature made him laugh
When dancing to a merry harp!

Under an overhanging crag,
He heard the roar from raging rapids,
Shadowed by an antlered stag,

Met some ghostly droning Druids,
He watched a wicker basket burn,
That appeased the Hunter Herne.

Down he went in Devil's Glen,
Waded through a weaving river,
Where he faced some little men
Beneath the bright moon's silver slither,
Then he reached for Lugh's spear
And felt his body quake with fear.

He went through mist, high on a hill,
Earth's green rings all girdled round,
Here at Tara, where time stood still,
He heard some music from underground;
There ancient voices, ever singing,
Praise and adore their Celtic King.

After he'd travelled around Ireland,
Found a sword set on a ridge,
Felt its power surge through his hand,
Now he'd crossed that ancient bridge.
He felt his pagan passions revive,
That made his soul so spring alive.

It dawned on him he'd been deceived,
Found he'd strayed off Pilgrims' Way,
He met Saint Patrick's spirit, who grieved,
Saw a vision when he prayed,
Fountains sprung forth sevenfold,
And saw a city burning in gold.

Sarah McKnee

Shepherdess on mountain path,
Such a sweet wee bonnie lass,
Known for her hearty laugh,
Proud upright and bold as brass,
Breezes ruffle her auburn hair,
Skipping through the flowery lea,
Humming a lively Scottish air,
This refined young Sarah McKnee.

When she hears the ravens nag,
Flying from a rugged rock,
Yonder she sights an antlered stag;
As she goes by lapping loch,
In her clan's bright tartan shirt,
With her soul so full of fire,
Passing by old haunted Kirk,
There she sees a phantom prior.

Just before a castle ruin,
Right at the bottom of the glen,
Where she meets a giggling goblin,
Standing near a dragon's den,
Then she senses its fiery breath,
Thinks about those legends of auld,
Gripped in icy presence of death
And it makes her blood run cold.

How she loves the alluring forest,
Bluebells spread out like a carpet,
Power of magic she seems to possess,
When she comes to an elfin fair,
Picks up a bunch of parsley and thyme,
As she enters fairies' hall,
Between the spruce and scented pine,
Shafts of golden sunlight fall.

On her way to Loch Ness,
Hears some angels strumming lyres,
In this place so full of zest;
When she comes to Falls at Fyers,
Revels in its raging roar,
Fast and furious, ceaseless flow,
Finds it makes her spirit soar
And it's girded with a rainbow.

She stares up at the eagle wings,
Gliding free; it fills her with zeal,
Every hill and mountain sings,
Time when heaven is so real;
Down on her way to the village,
Tosses and turns her pretty head,
As she crosses hump stone bridge,
Burn is bubbling in its bed.

Now she's stirred by blowing bagpipes,
Sustaining sound of fourths and fifths,
Folk tune soon scales its heights,
Scottish music so uplifts.
Dances her traditional steps,
Skilfully around those crossing swords,
When her feelings reach their depths,
She bows before those local lords.

Loch reflects the moon so round,
Where she spots a sparking spunkie,
Water wavers where travellers drown,
Thrown from a neighing kelpie,
She shudders at its beating hooves,
Riding over river and rill,
Rearing up this spectre of spooks,
That drives the dripping watermill.

Golden stars twinkle and peep,
She gazes into heaven's soul,
Lies there with her flock of sheep,
Counting shooting stars that roll;
After night takes off its cloak
And she wakes with huntsman's horn,
Plans the moment she'll elope,
Then she rises with the dawn.

English and Classical Culture

We pay a visit to beautiful Italy, experiencing its fascinating culture, and then move on to the stunning splendour and opulence of Versailles and its final downfall in the French Revolution.

T. S. Elliot described London as an 'unreal city' in 'The Waste Land'; here we also look at the darker side of this vibrant metropolis.

Count Lenatto

Count Lenatto never forgot that day,
He stood before his oval looking glass,
Saw his world in dreary shades of grey;
After baring his soul, removed his mask,
He vowed to follow evil all the way,
Through the power of aristocratic class,
With his soul clothed in Devil's disguise,
All the darkness shone so bright in his eyes.

At night his pair of hounds stood there on guard,
Later on he heard them give out a howl
When a demon crept through his cobbled courtyard,
Tu-whit! tu-whoo! came from a tawny owl.
He rose in bed and fear shot through his heart,
Those creaking stairs, then faced a fiend so foul
That entered through his open bedroom door,
And found it made his inward spirit soar.

He stared outside his window at that storm,
Received a spirit from hell's dark grey pit,
Gazed into the mirror at his sinister form;
Holding his silver-knobbed swagger stick,
He watched his dandy image being born,
Burst into an evil laughing fit;
Betrayed every movement he couldn't hide,
Stood there relishing in old-fashioned pride.

He passed some peasants working hard in the fields,
Drove on ahead in his black horse-drawn carriage
Along a mountain road, with rumbling wheels;
He cracked his whip and thundered over a bridge

Into a village, with time so hot on his heels,
Watched the sun peep down the mountain ridge,
Cursed those church bells, chiming down below,
And his journey ended by Lake Como.

All that week he dreamed about his Countess,
Helped her off the ferry onto the quay,
Admired her elegance in her long white dress,
The way she moved along so gracefully,
Her raven tresses fell on her heaving breast.
He offered his beloved his rose on bended knee,
Captured her heart with sophistication and charm,
Walked so proudly and took her upon his arm.

Then he took her back to his glorious mansion,
Through his gates, into his classical garden,
All the symmetry lifted up his pride,
Venus glistened in a gushing fountain,
Made his self and spirit spring alive.
He stared into the green and lofty mountains,
Enhanced the brilliant blue Italian sky,
And he saw an eagle soaring on high.

Often he went into the village to relax,
Watched peasants dancing round the streets
Wearing masks and bells and pointed hats;
This cavalcade of clowns with clumsy feet,
Letting off their noisy crackerjacks,
Those dazzling fireworks, in this holy week.
He stared at a saint's statue behind a priest,
Now seemed like a damp squib on this sacred feast.

At eight he went along the hall to dine,
Beneath some rainbow crystal chandeliers
Hanging above a table of food and wine.
He sat and entertained his many peers
With a string quartet that played divine,
Music that made his guests prick up their ears;
Although his eyes were fastened upon the Countess,
Wearing her sparkling heart-shaped diamond necklace.

Candelabra flickered in the breeze;
He watched Liszt playing his grand piano,
As his fingers stroked those black-and-white keys;
He pictured a flowery meadow all aglow,
Where he stroked a lamb upon his knees,
Beside a stream, listening to its flow;
This music echoed every pastoral scene,
Reliving past days when his soul was green.

He watched the maestro on the keyboard;
It felt like Dante's 'Inferno' being raised,
Heard the screams, so deep in hell that roared,
Feared he'd be lost forever in this maze.
Spellbound he rose to his feet to applaud
When Liszt's wild rhythms set his mind ablaze;
He moved into those realms of unbridled passion,
Driven and tormented by his indwelling demon.

Next day he met a priest astride his ass
On his way to San Martino chapel,
He followed him up a winding mountain pass,
Greeted by an ancient chiming bell,

He joined some people at the morning mass,
Fell under the Italian culture's spell,
Those Latin chants that linked his soul to Rome;
Found it being lifted before Satan's throne.

After his siesta in the afternoon shade,
Smirked at a mural of the Madonna and child,
Cursed this innocence he'd often craved;
Touched his depths within that became defiled,
Now haunted him like death beyond the grave,
As evil spirits drove his passions wild.
How he hated this wonderful work of art
That kept on stirring and taunting his stony heart.

He drove his carriage into the city of Milan,
To La Scala and watched Don Giovanni;
It froze his heart to see the fate of this man,
Now realised this could be his destiny.
He welcomed the cool air from his lady's fan,
That quenched his thoughts from the fires of eternity;
Throughout Mozart's moving opera he grieved,
Learned the way in which he'd been deceived.

Beneath some windy clouds in a moonlit sky,
His spirit felt as wild as the restless lake,
Thought about how life had passed him by,
Worried about that storm about to break,
Shunned the feeling 'what happens after you die',
He couldn't stop his sense of heartache
That he'd leave his life of luxury and leisure,
And lose all his power and sensual pleasure.

When he stood before the gates of hell,
Heard its deafening, roaring fiery furnace,
His voice echoed down a bottomless well,
Cringing at all the horrors he'd have to face;
Many terrors increased the farther he fell,
But trapped forever inside this dreadful place
He was tortured and whipped, shackled in chains,
There amongst the six-foot crackling flames.

The Sun King

Sun King prays inside his chapel,
Meditates upon heaven and hell,
After Matins goes his way;
Dressed in the fashion of his day,
Walking along in exquisite grace,
Stately pride lights up his face,
He stands there in his classical garden,
Right near Apollo's gushing fountain.
This glorious sight enhances his spirit;
Imagines he's sitting in a chariot,
Drawn by four white steeds through the sky,
Watching the sunrise over Versailles,
Reaching those heights of idolatry,
The only place he feels so free.

At night he continues to revel in self;
His sense of beauty, perfection and wealth,
Lanterns light up his chateau
Like fairy castles all aglow.
He passes statues of elves and fawns,
Burning torches shadow the lawns,
He hears his soldiers' kettledrums roll,
Trumpet blasts lift up his soul.
He watches fireworks whoosh in the air –
Crackling, sparkling everywhere,
Glittering on the rushing cascades,
Lighting those orange groves and glades.
His symbol covers the whole night sky,
Sprinkling stars over Versailles.

The Grand Masked Ball

Summer night at a Grand Masked Ball,
Chandeliers sparkle in the hall.
Beneath a classical painted ceiling,
Stands the celebrated Sun King
Among his aristocratic guests,
Richly attired in costume dress;
Fancy masks cover their faces,
Reflect inside the Galerie des Glaces.
An orchestra plays a minuet,
People dance in stately step,
In excellent courtly manners and taste;
Bow and curtsy face to face.
Around midnight the Sun King asks
Everybody to remove their masks,
Then clowns and harlequins appear;
The Devil with his pointed beard,
Sophisticated, all dressed in black,
Removes his dark three-cornered hat.
His green eyes glow, his face bright red
With two horns upon his head;
When he stamps his cloven hoof,
A genie rises into the roof.
Chandeliers play a Chinese scale
That drains the dancers' faces pale,
All spellbound by his feats of magic.
He waves his silver-topped swagger stick;
Clowns start juggling luminous balls
That flash and fly across the hall;
Harlequins do acrobats,
Now move swift as crackerjacks.

His troupe of demons dance in the night,
Into the garden's glowing moonlight,
Dancing with spirits upon smooth lawns
With Grecian gods, satyrs and fawns,
Shadowy wings that flash and flare,
From powerful princes of the air;
Enter above the dance room floor,
And makes the dancers' spirits soar,
Till they all become defiled,
Which drives their sense of order wild.
They begin to dance the Devil's Waltz,
And music beats in a demonic pulse;
Violins hit their dissonant heights,
Woodwind sounds like Pan's twin pipes.
The orchestra plays avant-garde,
Devil no longer hides his façade;
Now dressed in dazzling white,
Appears this time as an angel of light.
His demonic monks are singing in Latin,
All shine so bright in their height of sin,
Now blend with deities through time;
Return to monastery, church and shrine,
When the sun awakes the dawn,
They fade into that misty morn.

Madame Pompadour

The brilliant sunlit bright blue sky
Lights the grandiose garden at Versailles,
All laid out in symmetrical form,
Classical crests cut in the lawn,
Red and golden flowers in parterres,
Scenting the warm, fine summer air,
Impresses Madame Pompadour;
This beauty makes her spirit soar.
So proud being the king's mistress,
There in her blue embroidered dress.
Her body moves in elegance and grace,
Rosy cheeks highlight her face,
With lovely tresses of golden hair
Falling upon her bosom fair,
Her hat displays a scarlet plume;
Sets off her eighteenth century costume.
She meets her lover, this Queen of Hearts,
This lady refined in all the arts.

Petit Trianon

A thousand torches burn this night,
Bath a grotto in ethereal light,
Out of caves to rocky shelves,
Storm about eleven elves;
Hatred burns inside each elf,
Go on about their lack of wealth.
They peep between some foliage green,
Watch the Sun King and his queen
Parade around in glittering gowns,
Wear their sparkling golden crowns.
Elves join in this merry procession;
Acting around, like mischievous children,
Taunting the ladies, strumming their lutes,
Copy those clowns piping their flutes.
Keeping their spirits wide awake,
Enjoy this lively midsummer fete.
The elves keep on singing a song;
Echoes around the Petit Trianon,
Revolution so rife in trembling air,
They make the peasants' anger flare.

The Model Hamlet

Young Queen Marie Antoinette
Often goes to her model hamlet,
Walking along in elegant stride,
That touch of class she cannot hide,
Her flaxen hair tied in a bow,
Those rosy cheeks so fresh they glow,
By the watermill's dripping wheel
Rumbling round that rouses her zeal.
She watches pretty maidens by the leat,
Giggling and paddling their pretty feet.
She loves her herd of Swiss-bred cows,
Grazing under the leafy boughs;
She follows a milkmaid on the green,
Helps her make some pots of cream,
There in cool, white marble dairy.
She invites her in for afternoon tea,
Inside her green vine-covered cottage,
Right in the heart of her model village;
Imagines being a squire's wife,
Soak up the simple way of country life.

The Queen's Ghost

Two charming Oxford gentlewomen
Walk along the Petit Trianon
Late one August afternoon,
Sense a lady's fear and gloom,
Feel her presence as their guide;
Walks elegantly by their side.
They cross over a wooden bridge,
Come to the French Queen's model village,
Share those moments when time stands still,
When passing an old thatched watermill
Spinning its watery wheel of fate,
Churning up its bitterness and hate
Into those lazy summer streams;
They both can sense her broken dreams.
They find this difficult to digest,
That figure in a long white dress
Sitting down on a fine cut lawn,
Watching her features gradually form;
Her powdered face looks white with lead,
Fair hair fluffed on her forehead,
Curls are running down her back,
Above her shady little white hat.
Ladies turn the other way,
Their hearts are filled with disarray,
But face their biggest shock as yet
The painting of Marie Antoinette
Hanging inside a musty room,
Late one August afternoon,
Shocked this portrait matches her ghost,
That proved to be their perfect host.

The Execution

The revolution spirit hovered around Paris,
Creaking cartwheels rumbled down the street
Before the cheering hundreds of peasants waiting
To shake their fists and spit at the royal elite,
All gathered in a bloodthirsty crowd,
Angry that King Louis looked so proud.

They watched their sovereign tread the scaffold steps,
Listened to the military kettledrums roll,
Enjoyed the mounting tension that filled the air,
Inspired blood lust in every man's soul;
When the guillotine's blade came hurtling down,
Cut off the head that wore a stately crown.

The crowd poured scorn upon the Lord's anointed,
Kept on cheering over this sacrifice,
Gloating over Louis's severed head,
Set a stage for the coming Antichrist,
Spun the wheel of fortune and brought a curse,
Spread anarchy throughout the universe.

Evil spirits taunted the peasants in the city,
Soon found themselves gripped in death throes
And danced around like clowns at a carnival.
It whipped up a thousand wicked woes,
Unleashed the fury from the depths of hell
And every church sounded its funeral knell.

Nightmare in Hell

Horse riders chased me across a fiery plain,
I came to a quay and saw a ferryman
Pull hand over hand on a squeaking chain.

I watched his finger guide me where to stand,
Stepped onto his ferry to cross a lake,
So filled with fear as I approached this island,

Being driven on this journey of fate
By this fiend in his drooping, hooded cloak,
Through the jaws of hell so wide awake;

I heard the roar from its belly in its throat,
The smell of brimstone took away my breath,
Here among the flames and thick black smoke.

What torment I felt from this place of death
That glowed red inside just like a forge fire,
I was shaken when the ferry jolted left,

All the piercing screams that sounded so dire;
This torture plunged me in depths of despair,
Saw those corpses burn on a funeral pyre.

I flinched at demons cracking their whips in the air,
Lashing at broken bodies bound on a wheel,
Found this cruelty more than I could bear.

My shattered heart attempted to face this ordeal,
Struggled when I stepped onto the shore;
The air was stifling but I felt so full of zeal.

I feared I'd be a prisoner for evermore;
The ferryman haunted me with his evil laugh,
And I went inland and heard a mighty roar.

Regret overwhelmed me for taking this path,
Ventured farther into this darkened dell,
I gripped tightly onto my pilgrim's staff.

Then I glared in the flaming pit of hell,
Its rumbling bowels thundered around my head;
I turned and heard a tolling funeral bell,

Saw ghostly monks, those spirits of the dead
Singing plainchant, that sounded so full of woe,
Their faces looked gaunt, their eyes glowed red.

I watched them swing their censers to and fro,
Soon set those wicked forces of darkness free,
That came out of a shrine with faces aglow;

And found my spirit gripped by this idolatry
That shook my body down to the soles of my feet;
I realized how this ritual had affected me.

Eventually I found myself in a street
In town, riddled with death, famine and disease;
I kept wondering to myself, "What more could I meet?"

I hated the stench of brimstone on the breeze,
That shadow of gloom present on every face,
Pale as the stark dead branches on the trees.

Later I came to a crowded marketplace,
Watched clowns and magicians perform on stage;
Their black magic made me flee in haste.

I cursed bloodlust this crowd all seemed to crave,
Watching heads fall off an axe's block,
Then thrown down into a greedy grave.

I passed some shaking skeletons, screaming in stocks,
As I walked straight up to Hangman's Hill;
Stood under the scaffold, there at the top,

Heard some voices screaming under a grill,
Echoed from deep, dark dungeons underground;
Saw their bodies being ground in a mill.

I fled to a Gothic castle, high on a mound,
Heard the clanking chains of a portcullis
And a creaking drawbridge lowered down.

Down in a moat I heard some serpents hiss,
Crossed a drawbridge into a courtyard,
When a figure approached me in the mist.

A burning torch lit up his face, so scarred,
Increased my fear and tension even more,
Now the steel portcullis crashed and jarred.

I grabbed his key, unlocked a creaking door,
Met hundreds of knights in a banqueting hall;
Covered in strands of cobwebs and waiting for war.

I saw the shadows of knights move on the wall,
When a demon blew into a ram's horn
And those fiends soon obeyed the battle call.

I waited in this place, my heart all filled with scorn,
Rushed to those restless horses there outside,
I rode in the blinding flashes of a storm.

What power I felt from the horsemen's evil pride;
Their whips of lightning split the air asunder,
Thrill of horses galloping side by side,

To hear their thudding hoof-beats in the thunder.
I rode with demonic empires that rose and fell,
With two hundred million that rose in wonder,

Straight out of the roaring abyss in hell;
Saw how its furnace enhanced the scarlet sky.
Now I'd fallen under its wicked spell,

On a par with gods, so exalted was I,
Made me shine much brighter than the sun,
My soul power had never soared so high.

Somehow I knew I'd reached the end of my run,
Shocked to see Satan fall in a thunder flash,
And the forces of darkness were overcome.

I saw the sparks fly when the weapons clashed,
How the cherubim swords all gleamed with light,
And the pride of the Devil's horsemen smashed.

My heart and demonic knights here at their height
Were cast down to join the eternal dead
In the lake of fire that glowed so bright.

But I landed with such a thump upon my bed,
Relieved the evil nightmare of hell had fled.

The Black Forest

Thunder and lightning awake the red dawn,
In this dark land of the giants in a storm,
Where their ancient feet have trodden
Through those haunts of their Saxon god, Woden;
Seeing his ship with its sail on the lake,
Under the heavens that start to shake.
Once on the shore, he's seen mounting his horse,
Swinging its hooves with incredible force,
Followed by howling bloodhounds in the sky,
Valkyries' swords that are glowing on high,
Glimpsing the eagle's wide wings that soar,
Over those mountains where waterfalls roar,
Lead to a river that's running in zest,
Here in the heart of the Black Forest.

Sunshine now spreads its most glorious beams,
Flashes its feeling on clear, rippling streams,
Lights up the lake like a silver bowl;
Watch how it mirrors the mountains' grand soul!
Brightens those lambs on the greenest of hills,
Captures the skylark that's piping its trills,
Birds and the bees make their summery sound
Under the sun that is glowing and round.
Freyja's fine features that light up her face,
Wearing her glittering golden necklace,
Shining green eyes – what a sight to behold! –
Standing there crying her tears of red gold;
Glinting long tresses of coppery hair
Fall on the breast of this goddess so fair;
Singing high voice, how it soars like a falcon,
Echoing through the lush valley and mountain,

Stirring those nymphs and shepherds alike,
Musing the sun at its sweltering height,
Sparkling on the rivers in zest,
Here in the heart of the Black Forest.

Red sun now darkens the evening tide,
Laid back old moon like grim reaper's scythe,
Bearded giant fiend by a dripping dark cave,
Right where the wandering sprits all rave,
From those broken dry bones near a bridge,
There in the region beyond an old village,
Where this foul creature spilt so much blood,
Thor killed this troll with a mighty great thud,
With a swing from his heavy stone hammer,
Rapturous cheers shake the towers in Valhalla,
Overlooks the river that's running in zest,
Here in the heart of the Black Forest.

Midnight chimes from the monastery bell,
Bringing about this Valpurgis night spell,
Ritual fires blazing on mountaintops;
Hark, how it crackles and snaps and it pops!
Whispering witches, see how they zoom
On their broomsticks beneath the horned moon,
Looking down on the old sleeping town,
Laughing at ghouls that are gathered around,
Coming down on the mountain's high place,
Meeting the Devil there face to face;
Shows off his shining black cloven hooves,
Joins in the dance with the witches and spooks;
Moving around with their frenzied feet,
Capture the rhythms of demonic beat.

Old hags are riding on goats from the woods,
Druids start droning in drooping white hoods,
Gather in a circle between the raging fires,
Hearing voices from dissonant choirs,
Brethren of air, how they flash and they crack,
Lucifer's worshippers taken aback,
Purple red clouds formed in the twilight
Of the gods that are beaming so bright,
Fairy and elfin dark kingdoms all glow,
Princes and powers of the air, how they flow
From the imperial glory of Rome,
Bearded red sun now sits on its throne,
Reddens the rivers all running with zest,
Here in the heart of the Black Forest.

Question of Time

Grandfather clock,
Pendulum swings,
Tick and a tock,
Sometimes it rings.
Quarterly chime,
Hourly it gongs
Moving through time,
Dings and it dongs.
Military clock,
Rising at seven,
Right on the dot,
Bed at eleven,
Twenty past three
Feet in the hall,
Who can it be?
Shadow on wall,
Knock on the door,
Switch on the light,
Quarter to four,
Hell of a fright!
Dining with time,
Tick and a tock,
Destiny's mine,
Grandfather clock,
Stop –
Eternity!

Steam Train Journey

I'm a steam train, there in the station,
Raring to go, puffing my steam,
Puff – puff – puff – puff,
Going along, gathering speed,
Over the points, quarter to nine,
Straight down the line, destiny time.
Fireman is there, shovelling the coal,
Stoking my fire, good for my soul,
Sounding the whistle, steaming the breeze,
Cows in the fields, rooks in the trees,
Passenger train, going so fast,
Opposite way, making me sway,
Goes in my mind, into my past,
Memories taunt, feeling the strain,
Fanning my flames, hammers my brain.
Signal's on red, straight up ahead,
Slowing me down, slowing me down,
Grinds to a halt, stopping me dead,
Signal's on green, signal's on green,
Ready to go, puffing my steam,
Puff – puff – puff – puff,
Going along, gathering speed,
Puffing my steam, out of my funnel,
Woof – woof – woof – woof,
Round a sharp bend, into a tunnel,
Darkness and gloom, dark as a tomb,
Journey in hell, lit up in red,
Cathedral cave, demons all rave,
Over a bridge, on a dark ridge,
Sky like a forge, lava in gorge,
Bubbling in lake, blazing in red,
Seeing the demons, ferry the dead.

Lightning on plains, feeding the flames,
Tormented folk, screaming in chains,
Nerves all on edge, high on a ledge,
Sweating my steam, out of my funnel,
Seeing the light, end of the tunnel,
Sun's all in gold, clouds all unfold,
Meadows are green, monastery seen,
Ruins all soar, fills me with awe,
Ghostly nuns choir, fuels me with fire,
Good for my soul, feeling divine,
Straight down the line, destiny time,
Fading away, end of the day,
Fading away, fading away,
Fading away, fading away.

That Garden

One day I walked through a garden,
Fashioned in fruits of golden light,
Thought I'd found the key to heaven,
Glad I'd fled from the darkness of night.
The tree of knowledge of good and evil,
With fruits so tempting, beyond compare,
Deceived by that serpent the Devil;
His sophistry caught me unaware.
I plucked and ate forbidden fruit,
Knew that black would now be white,
Now this evil had taken root,
My idolatry had reached its height.
The garden faded, I'd become wise,
Now the serpent had shed its disguise.

Natural Rebirth

Glorious sunshine fills the sky,
Focus where I and my love do lie,
We are naked in this solitude,
Heaven's creation supplies the food.
Under foliage so fresh and green,
Where no finer shade is seen,
We hear the garden's own heartbeat,
Taste its glowing fruits so sweet,
From those apples on the trees,
Its fragrance carried on the breeze.
We watch the weaving stream trickling
By and hear its spirit sing.
We rest in the breast of Mother Earth,
And both enjoy nature's rebirth.

Elizabethan Song

Catherine stared in the blushing summer sky
That glowed over her fragrant rose garden,
She opened her window and began to cry,
Dreamt about last night's moonlit fountain,
Where she'd heard her lover sing with his lute,
That filled her heart so deep with love's content.
Inside her garden, she found her thoughts took root,
Her dancing feet displayed her merriment.
She stooped to pick some parsley, thyme and sage,
Moved between those beds of healing herbs,
Enjoyed those moments in this golden age;
All those enchanting notes from singing birds,
There's no other place she'd rather be –
For love now ruled her heart and set it free.

First Love

One day a charming Georgian gentleman
Drew buckets of water from his red-roofed well,
Watered his damask roses that graced his garden,
Near where the golden shafts of sunlight fell.
He sniffed his blooms, much sweeter than incense,
When he heard some fast hoof-beats approach;
Thought about his beloved's countenance,
He helped her step down off her stately coach,
Embraced and walked with her, arm in arm,
Beneath the blazing, bright, blue summer skies,
Overcome by her gentle ladylike charm
When he gazed into her dark brown eyes;
His first love seemed like a never-ending dream,
Here in his garden, when his soul was green.

The Age of Oliver Cromwell

A spire church overlooked the river
At the village in Hemingford Grey;
Peasants worked hard in the fields,
Shepherding their sheep this springtime day;
When they rested from their labour,
Enjoyed a cool afternoon snooze,
Underneath some weeping willows
That shaded the lazy River Ouse.

Puritans roamed round the village;
Stood upright so stiff and proud,
Holding their black-bound bibles,
Mingled with a gathering crowd.
They wore their tall black-brimmed hats,
With golden buckles on their shoes,
Stepped forward, opened their bibles;
They preached on their religious views.

The Christian roundheads went to war,
Angered the princes and powers of the air
When Cromwell cleansed the English churches
And demons left in a flash and flare.
He smote those idols with his sword;
Rejoiced in spirit as pagan heads fell,
Whitewashed murals on the walls,
Images inspired from torment in hell.

A Cavalier lady strolled in the meadows,
Her blue dress brushed on the grass,
Grace displayed in her deportment;
Bore the air of a superior class.

Those fine features of her face
Belong to those of an aristocrat;
Her exquisite velvet silk and lace,
And a scarlet plume upon her hat.

This lady met her Cavalier soldier,
Walked along in elegance and grace;
He stroked his little pointed beard,
Bore a devilish grin on his face.
His black curls rested on his shoulders,
Looked handsome, so dashing and refined,
Always dressed in the latest fashions;
Thought he was a gift to mankind.

Cromwell's army gathered at Naseby,
His cavalry and troops looked so inspired,
Pikemen all geared up for action,
When the cannons and muskets fired;
Time soon came for the cavalry charge,
Their horses' hooves made such a thud;
Puritans drew their flashing swords,
Sought and spilt the Cavaliers' blood.

Those 'dunkings' in village ponds;
Many innocent women were drowned.
All the supposed guilty were hung,
Proved the Devil's reason was sound.
Witchfinder General, Matthew Hopkins,
Watched so many witches hanged;
People thought this purged their sins
And hysteria burned throughout our land.

Now King Charles' head had rolled,
Cromwell had set this England free,
He became known as Lord Protector,
And fought against all idolatry,
Lived by what the scriptures told,
Which proved to keep his country safe;
He did as those prophets of old
And he lived his life in faith.

My Lady

You move like an ever wandering stream,
Like sparkling crystal waters divine;
Your heart is soft, like a fragrant white rose,
Just like the purity within your soul.
How I long to gaze in your eyes,
See that precious heavenly virtue
That lasts for evermore, My Lady.

I also know you're a thriving actress,
Shining there in those theatre lights;
You excel in arts of coquetry.
I'm captive to your cruel yet charming heart;
Yes, I alone am your audience.
My throat is dry and my skin is moist;
Your passion brings me alive, My Lady.

Northumbrian Coast

Warlike demons invoked a howling tempest,
Stirred up every spirit and ghost,
Darkened many caverns, caves and coves,
There on the Northumbrian coast.

Bamburgh Castle sat high above a rock,
Where some flying dragons roared,
Spewed their streaming flames of fire in fury,
Were cursed in time for evermore.

A gusty ill north wind silvered the grass,
Over miles of golden sand dunes,
Aroused those Saxon voices from long ago;
Spoke in riddles from buried runes.

Giant waves lashed on rocks black as a cauldron,
Whipped up gathering froth and foam,
Just like a wicked witch seething with anger,
That made those sheer cliffs creak and groan.

Beneath the Dunstanburgh Castle ruins,
Those raging billows fared so bold,
A ghostly maiden screamed in the dungeon,
Soon woke those wandering knights of old.

Old hags rode their broomsticks to Emberton Crags,
All casting their evil spells in turn,
Laughed and blurted out their wicked rhymes,
They danced beside a restless burn.

Surging waves soon reached Holy Island,
Threatened to swamp the steadfast hermit;
Saint Cuthbert raised his holy hand,
He stilled the soaring sea's wild spirit.

All around Lindisfarne monastery,
Ancient plainchant sang profound,
Sacred music brought such peace and calm
To listening ears all gathered round.

Day of the Fairies and Elves

A traveller opened a mossy gate,
Went through a wood at Seathwaite,
Glimpsed an elf that looked so sullen,
Down by the rippling River Duddon.
He followed him over some stepping stones,
Listening to his moans and groans;
Then he crouched well down in the brake
To see which magic path he'd take.
It ducked in a spiral tunnel of green,
Heightened by the sunlight's beam,
There on a glittering garden so bright,
With floating golden orbs of light,
Started to sparkle, flash then crack,
Which stopped his early afternoon nap.
This hiker could hardly believe his eyes
When fairies flew round like butterflies,
With open, golden whirring wings;
Lit up the elves by silvery springs,
Bubbled beneath a humped stone bridge,
Here in the heart of an elfin village.

Absorbed and gripped by this fairy tale,
He watched the elves drinking ale;
Looked so mean, with hunched up backs,
Wore their green bedraggled hats,
All bearded faces, red as roses,
Pointed ears and turned up noses,
Blew froth from their tankards of beer,
All followed by a hearty cheer;
Stamped in their winkle picker shoes,
Seemed hell-bent on airing their views.

He heard trumpets on the village green,
Elves all cheered their king and queen;
There in sparkling, golden crowns,
They paraded around in purple gowns.
He saw them open a summer fair;
Roaring voices filled the air.
He watched the elves enjoy their games,
Fire-eater swallowed up his flames,
Jugglers and puffed-up, prancing clowns;
Harlequins skipped upon the mounds,
Children did their head-over-heels,
Rolling and sparking like Catherine wheels;
Light flowed from these girls and boys,
That captured their former heavenly joys.

He came to Wallowbarrow Crag,
Watched the circling ravens nag.
Above in the skies, turning grey,
A buzzard swooped down on its prey.
Here he met the goblin race,
With presence of anger on every face;
Sometimes they sneered, sometimes they frowned,
Bore their teeth, all flat and ground.
They stomped so firm with marching feet,
All in step with a demonic beat,
Down an ancient path that glowed;
They each looked like a puffed-up toad.
He heard those goblins stamp on the bridge,
On their way to the elfin village;
Their leaders, armed with shields and swords,
Strutted around like little lords,

The peasants had pitchforks and knives,
They wielded their axes, chains and scythes.
Fairies appeared in a heavenly glow,
Blinded those goblins down below;
Slashed at each other all in vain,
Ended up wounded, screaming in pain
On the ground, all out of puff,
Smitten and beaten, all ends up.
He saw the elves dart here and there,
Seemed to appear from everywhere;
Kicked those goblins up the bum,
So bent on having mischief and fun.
They let out three big hearty cheers,
Plucked hairs out of the goblins' beards,
Jumped hard on their bare pot bellies,
Rolled around like fresh set jellies.
How he laughed at this amusing sight
That faded away in the morning light.

London Town

London Town, so full of surprises,
City stretches and gives a yawn
When the morning curtain rises;
Welcome in that sunlit dawn.
Hark, how the stream of traffic drones,
Constant and busy as a hive,
Underground trains in catacombs,
Streets and roads all buzzing alive.

The view from Westminster Bridge
Overlooks historic buildings and spires,
While foghorns sound from boats and barges
On serpentine Thames that never tires;
How this misty river soars
Through London Bridge's giant twin towers,
Opening up its mighty jaws,
Every single vessel it devours!

Still stately houses of parliament,
Just like the British stiff upper lip,
Once gave birth to British Empire;
Now seems no more than a passing ship.
Big Ben stands straight to attention,
Its huge bell sounds its solemn chime,
Sees things past and things to come,
Like London's heart beating through time.
The shadow from the ghostly statesman
Puffing merrily away at his cigar,
Steeped so deeply in druidic order;
Did he take his beliefs too far?

This high profile figure at war,
Raving there, this rampant bulldog,
Charged like a fearsome wild boar,
His words exalted just like a god.

Eyes all down on the royal ritual,
Clockwork changing of the guard;
Here we reach the height of tradition,
All stark and straight up as the Shard.
Kettledrums roll and marching feet,
Makes hairs stand on back of the hand,
When music comes in on the beat,
It blazes from Grenadier Guards Band.
Horses clopping in regal stride,
Golden coach moves along the royal mile,
Queen's on her way to Buckingham Palace,
Now waves from her window with a smile.

Splendour of Westminster Abbey,
Listen to the organ's sound,
Sheer grandeur of Gothic pillars,
Arched, rising from holy ground,
Music echoes in ribbed domed roof,
Captures the nation's hopes and dreams,
The black-and-white floor of the aisle –
Hark, footsteps of kings and queens!

Round and round the Tower of London,
A dozen ravens squawk and glide
Above the Tudor gardens of death,
Reflect its darker secrets inside,

In the severe-looking edifice,
Once where monarchs' heads did fall,
Now houses the sparkling crown jewels,
But pain's still imprisoned within each wall.

Nelson's so firm upon his column,
Looks down on Trafalgar Square,
Where the four Babylon lions
Give it all a superior air.
There along with gushing fountains,
New Year's Eve crowds gather here,
Indulge in champagne celebrations,
Welcome in the brand new year.

Thousands of excited shoppers,
Tread the pavements of Oxford Street,
Pass by shop window displays;
That sound of never-ending feet.
Financial wizards at the stock exchange,
In their flashes of genius they trust,
Eying up their computer screens,
See if the markets will boom or bust!

Those printing presses in Fleet Street,
Airing their views on celebrities,
Washing their dirty linen in public,
Iron out their faults and fallacies.
Wealthy bankers all sweetness and sugar,
These toffee-nosed, stuck up fat cats,
Now sit with bulging bellies like Buddha,
Become the nation's aristocrats.

Those swinging sixties in Carnaby Street,
David Bailey, Twiggy, the Shrimp,
Camera's flash, highlights in fashion,
Possess the energy of an imp.
Shakespeare's Globe, gaiety theatres,
Orchestras in Royal Albert Hall,
Splendid musical spectacular,
Raises the roof and gives its all.

Far away from hustle and bustle,
The parks so full of nature and zest,
With sunlight simmering on the lake;
Here the city man finds his rest.
Gathering crowds in Hyde Park,
Atheist rants through megaphone
Promoting his racist evolution,
This brainwashed bias set in stone.

Godly scholars from the past
Groan and turn inside the grave
At those puffed-up think tanks,
The way in which they all behave,
Those multicultural paths they tread,
These liberals deceived by sophistry,
Have us believe that God is dead,
Estrange mankind from eternity.

Hordes of red buses and black taxis
Whizzing round Piccadilly Circus,
Roaring traffic, swift as a leopard,
Passing Greece's statue of Eros,

West End's coloured lighting at night,
City's energy, all in the hub,
Its entertainment and its hype,
Here in cinema, casino, nightclub.

Those meetings in Masonic Hall
With black-and-white chequered floor,
Blindfolded and feigned hanged man,
They're bound to ritual for evermore.
Come, meet the city's darker side,
Moral yet deep into the occult,
Just as urbane as Jekyll and Hyde,
Sure as death lies in its vault.

Underneath the purring gas lamps,
Voice called out to Mary Clarke,
Jack the Ripper in swirling fog,
Masonic depths that proved so dark.
He carved those compasses on courtesan's face
From his evil ritual knife,
Wrote some graffiti on the wall,
That power of death over life.

When the great fire raged through London,
Crackling like lightning flashes,
Left skeleton black-and-white buildings
And from its heap of dust and ashes
Rose Christopher Wren's legendry phoenix,
This architect and Master Mason,
His temple bar gate, the key to the city,
He committed the vilest sin;

Now demonic wings overshadow
Five churches that form a pentagram,
Right in its centre stands Saint Paul's;
He tuned into this cosmic sham,

Straight up from the dragon's den,
This area is his counterfeit
Of the New Jerusalem,
End time's Antichrist's seat.
The Roman-Celtic London stone
Holds the city under its spell,
From the Vatican inside Rome,
Now stirs the beast chained up in hell.

Now we turn to the temple church,
Ghostly Templar in hooded cloaks,
Dancing to the cosmic beat,
Like Druids among the springs and oaks,
Embrace the highest Celtic deity,
Commune with sacrificial dead,
Gather round into a circle,
Worship Bran's glowing head.

As in the days of Queen Boudicea,
Touched by Belenos, sun god of fire,
Druid priests still instil this fear,
Its victims scream from a funeral pyre.
Mithraic temples under the earth,
Paganism still burns in British souls,
Still filters down to modern culture,
Just like glowing red hot coals.

Left wing driven Persian Bear,
Seeking whom it may devour,
Bringer of light in this fanfare,
Crushes in the wake of its sheer power.
It prowls around alone in the streets,
Growls from underground,
From the surging River Fleet,
That flows beneath old London town.

The famous bard's unreal city,
Where ancient feet have trod,
Protectors of the metropolis,
Wicker giants, Gog and Magog,
Parade in procession through the streets,
These bearers of the satanic light,
Hit the heights of sophistication,
White is black and black is white.

Circle of life from the London Eye
Spins round like a Catherine wheel,
Flashing its lights high in the sky,
Shows off the city's zip and zeal;
Masonic compass at its centre,
It's time to bring the curtain down;
Now the city has taken its bow,
Here in dear old London Town.

Medieval City

The spokes of the Western wheel's dazzling rays
Took me way back into old England.
My mind spun round and round in a maze

When I saw some wolves ravaging a lamb,
Heard them howl, that haunted the mountains and hills,
As I followed a path, from cairn to cairn,

And stared a while at the restless silver rills
Flashing on the rocky slopes all round,
Then found myself inside Dungeon's Ghyll.

I stood here like a prisoner, all chained and bound
To such beauty, where a waterfall roared
And I felt its rhythms shake the ground.

I came to the Harrison Stickle, where ravens cawed,
And wondered if this omen would bring me harm,
But after I climbed Jack's Rake, my spirit soared

Over those waters of a wavering tarn,
Where the lofty mountains inspired my grandeur;
Here at last my soul found peace and calm.

I roamed around in this wilderness of nature,
Searched around for the medieval mystery,
Went on my way and never felt so sure,

For deep in my heart I held that golden key
To unlock those memories from long ago;
Legend had urged me go into that city.

I wandered on; my heart was full of woe,
Towards the sun that rested on the ridge,
And felt a presence of some evil foe,

When I walked straight through a Lakeland village,
Came where waters surged in a bubbling beck
And I crossed over a humped stone bridge.

A hooded monk approached me from my left,
Beckoned me with his long, white skeleton finger;
I followed him close behind, from step to step,

Climbed a crooked path, that went higher and higher;
Deep in an abyss I saw the city of cities,
Overcome by its magnitude and horror.

I felt its people nursed a thousand pities
There beneath a blanket of smouldering brimstone,
And heard their sombre songs from their psalteries.

This tormented people looked all skin and bone,
Their ancient songs hammered in my brain;
Its pitch soon raised my tension up a tone,

To see the musicians shackled up in chains;
Suddenly everywhere blazed like a fiery furnace,
I saw nowhere to flee from rising flames

And smoke had formed into a demon's face,
Which sent cold shivers running down my back.
I saw the power of hell unleashed from this place;

When the dome of heaven began to crack,
I stood on a ledge and looked in a precipice
And found my way into the city off track.

The atmosphere soon gripped me like a vice;
As I walked along its medieval streets,
I faced the glowing eyes of rats and mice.

I followed some monks walking in sandalled feet,
Going down in procession to the abbey,
Along to worship in this unholy week.

I listened to plainchant sung in disharmony,
A smoking censer swung from the gothic roof,
And its fragrance almost overwhelmed me.

Some hairy fiend appeared with cloven hoof,
Sang the demonic black mass all in Latin;
I soon began to learn the bitter truth.

The censer burst and bats made such a din,
When that icy bell struck the midnight hour,
In this place that committed the ultimate sin.

I felt as though my soul had turned all sour
When a sense of oppression stifled the air,
That caught me in its overwhelming power.

Somehow I found myself in a city square
Where beggars and cripples laid round half-dead;
All the folk seemed to realise I was there,

Where a sense of torment and hatred had spread,
Soon chased after by this unholy mob;
Ran for my life, my feet felt heavy as lead.

At last I lost them, but so many streets I'd trod,
Wondered how to get out of this place in hell,
Sulphur fumes almost choked me in the fog.

At the last stroke from the abbey's bell,
Found I was free from that city of 'I be',
Woke from this bad nightmare and broke its spell;

And left the perils of that wicked city,
Escaped the yoke of the medieval mould,
Found that nothing would thwart my destiny:

I stood on a ridge and saw a city of gold.

Duddon Valley

Old spirits snapped their chains
   in dripping Dungeon's Ghyll,
Went on whining and wailing through the Wyrnose Pass,
Unlocking images from years ago, in the Duddon Valley,
And sunlight sparkled on the waters like polished glass.

Romans crossed some stepping stones set in this river,
Lifting their eagle banner high, that drove them forth,
Reviving terrors committed against Celtic warriors;
Ghostly Roman legions conquered Britain in the north.

Hearne the Hunter's hounds were howling in a forest,
Their glowing yellow eyes all glaring down the ages.
Druids bowed down before their serpent stone;
They heaped their wicked curses by the river that rages.

Skies were red and tinted purple as heather,
Druids' magic moved on its way, swift as Merlin;
Brooding dark clouds soon brewed some foul weather
That captured the spirit of war in wild ancient Britain.

Mars, the god of war, used thunder and lightning,
That flashed over the ever raging riverbed,
Weapons of war heard clashing in the Duddon Valley,
And scores and scores of British warriors lay there dead.

Stalemate

A powerful king sat on his throne
With his white knights gathered round,
A jackdaw pinched a precious stone
There in his glittering golden crown.

He moved his peasants just like pawns,
Decreed that all must lend a hand,
Had them search from dawn to dusk,
Which caused uprising through his land.

High on his horse, he's ready to fight,
Clad in armour, with sword and shield;
He searched throughout that day and night
And he forced two black knights to yield.

He met his bishop in his mitre,
Standing there in his purple robe,
He told him straight where next to move,
Not to kick against the goad.

Later he came to a shady wood,
Stopped to drink from a bubbling spring,
And saw a reflection of a lady,
Right near a glowing fairy ring.

He became besotted with this princess,
Dressed stylishly in her emerald green,
With golden hair and heaving breast,
He asked her to serve as sovereign queen.

A drawbridge lowered down from his castle;
He watched his army of dazzling knights
Rally at once to his command,
All mustered to engage in the fight.

The king decided on all-out attack,
The divine fought against dark fate;
He'd never faced an army so black,
The battle was locked in stalemate.

Inside a chapel he saw a dove
Lead him straight to a jackdaw's bones,
So glad of guidance sent from above
That pointed him to his missing stone.

Hymns of Apollo

Apollo stands in the sunlight's glare,
Shines on his locks of golden hair;
He sits and plucks his tuneful lyre,
His music burns with prophetic fire,
Making the meadows glow like a dream
While his melodies flow downstream,
Weave along until they cascade,
Echo round a leafy glade,
Reflect these visions of this seer
Inside a pool that mirrors clear.
Apollo appears from a wooded slope,
Meets the shepherds filled with hope;
Girls adorned in yellow flowers
Shine like gold in Apollo's powers.
His spirit pierces those realms of time,
Resound through the mountains so divine;
Gods of Delphi capture his fire,
Singing hymns from his tuneful lyre.

A Spring Morning

What pleasure golden sunlight brings!
Pegasus drinks from bubbling springs,
Distant mountains are icy blue,
Flowery meadows sparkle with dew.
Nymphs and shepherds are everywhere,
Dance around in springtime air;
Rustic sound of Pan's twin pipes,
Each young shepherd's soul delights.
Green hills covered with sheep and goats,
Pan keeps piping his tuneful notes;
His magic shades of high-pitched sound
Make the trees and flowers bow down;
How this enchanting music roves,
That finds its way in sacred groves!

Wine Festival of Bacchus

Summer shades of evening fall
On marble steps at Bacchus hall;
He lurks around in his garden glades,
Ivy clings to his colonnades.
He admires delicate young girls;
Weaving vine leaves in his curls,
He puts his ivy crown on his head,
Grabs his thyrsus off his bed,
Puts on his long dark purple robe,
Wanders into an ancient grove,
Drinks from a chalice he holds in his hand,
That inspires his festival through the land.
Nymphs and shepherds gather round,
Each one wears a ritual crown,
Dancing with satyrs on mountain's green;
Lively nymphs jump out of a stream,
Join these Bacchanalian delights,
Lift their spirits to dizzy heights.
The flutes all sound and timbrels beat,
Everyone dances with frenzied feet,
Enjoy their passions that all run wild;
Now all their souls have been defiled,
Drunk in the spirit from Bacchus's wine,
That pierces nature and realms of time.

Sea Nymphs

The Aegean Sea looks so blue,
Grecian isles all come in view,
Sea nymphs basking on the rocks,
Combing through their raven locks.
They take hold of each other's hands
And dance upon the golden sands.
They stop and thread their pearly beads,
Then ride upon the waves' white steeds,
Glancing down at the garden beneath,
Its plants that hug the coral reef,
They peep inside Neptune's caves,
Here in his kingdom under the waves.
When they hear him blowing his horn,
Watch the angry dark clouds form,
Feel the floors of sea vibrate
And restless giant billows break,
In fury on the rocky shore,
Where they hear the Roman god roar;
See lightning flash on his trident prongs,
Nymphs start singing their siren songs,
Riding on seahorses so high,
While thunder echoes through the sky,
There among the raging foam,
Swimming near him on his throne,
They're dazzled by his glittering crown,
Where the sea's emotions resound,
Here in the height of Neptune's power,
They're in time with his triumphant hour.

Curse of El Dorado

A curse if she should ever be found,
Spanish galleon that ran aground
Among the rocks on this rugged isle
Where ghostly Spanish seamen smile,
Bellowing out their woeful cries,
Curse those gulls that fall from the skies.
A bright sun bleaches that rotten deck,
Seaweed hangs around the wreck,
Clusters of barnacles hug its hull
Beneath the captain's glowing skull,
But deep inside the galleon's hold
Lie open chests of gleaming gold,
The curse that killed Captain Pedro;
He found the gold of El Dorado.

Cursed in Eternity

A Spanish galleon reels in the Bay of Biscay,
Heaves up and down on a stormy sea,
Thunder and lightning flashes point its way,
Light the galleon, cursed in eternity.

Wild waves wash over the wooden deck,
Soak the swaying captain, who grips his helm;
Tempts to steer his ship from becoming a wreck,
But finds he's entered into the Devil's realm.

Captain Pedro ignores his screaming slaves
Rattling their chains way down in that dark, deep hold,
Curses the northwest wind and sea that raves,
That soaks those shivering slaves with damp and cold.

Driving rain drips down the reeling mast,
Straining its ropes and rigging that snap in two;
Songs from ghostly sailors sound from the past,
Strike terrors in the hearts of this bloodthirsty crew.

It rises up fifteen fathoms, covered in foam,
A giant, green, slithering sea serpent that mocks,
Then stalks the swaying ship wherever it roams,
Which smashes to smithereens on some rocks.

An Alpine Tale

Beneath the overhanging crag,
A girl skipped down a mountain track,
Swished around in peasant's clothes
With black curls flowing down her back.

Majestic mountains lifted her spirit,
Mirrored in emerald lake below;
She watched a golden eagle soar,
There above those peaks of snow.

She heard those cowbells lower down,
Caught the smell of freshly felled pine,
Stopped to pick flowers from the valley,
Then put them in a holy shrine.

How hard she worked in those summer meadows,
Swept her scythe in the scorching sun,
Although sweat dripped down her face,
She sang old songs in her mother tongue.

One night she went to a village dance,
All dressed up in national costume,
Danced around with a young hunter,
Her flowering love began to bloom.

Her bright green dress and petticoat flared,
Delighted with every twist and turn;
When she gazed in the crackling bonfire,
It made her Slavonic passions burn.

Later she found herself abandoned,
When he spurned her tender love
And defiled her innocent nature,
Once like a dove sent from above.

Under the darkening, gathering clouds,
She heard the mighty thunder roll,
Watched the seven lightning forks
Strike like anger in her soul.

Driving rain came down in torrents,
Soaked her body right to the skin;
Her broken heart was bent on evil
From her sorrow that nagged within.

She went along to a witch's chalet
Upon a lonely mountain path,
Met a middle-aged old hag,
Froze when she heard her croaky laugh.

When she stepped into her kitchen,
Watched her bellows fan the flames,
Toads squealed from the bubbling cauldron
There in a fire on hanging chains.

The young girl embraced that wicked witch,
Begged her to cast an evil spell,
Then recited her words in rhyme,
Found it evoked some ogre from hell.

She followed her lover through a forest,
And a werewolf took him by surprise;
She's so stunned by the deed she's done,
Shocked she's now a devil in disguise.

This peasant girl, now full of grief
When she found him lying in mud,
Drew him closer to her bosom,
Which soaked her lacy blouse in blood.

She ran and jumped straight off a cliff,
Where a raging river roared,
Her body dashed on jagged rocks,
Where some circling black ravens cawed.

Diary of an Edwardian Lady

Edith, an Edwardian lady, walks
Stately through those springtime meadows,
In her ankle-length white dress
That brushes a carpet of wild flowers.
She stops a moment to untie her bun,
Letting her hair flow down her back,
Stoops down low on a riverbank,
There by a cluster of sweet violets.

Inside her cottage she does her paintings
And drawings, in pages of her diary,
Of wild flowers found on her nature walks;
She recites some poems that sing in her soul.

Down by the serpentine Thames,
She leans right over the water's edge,
Reaches for some horse chestnut buds,
Falls into the river and drowns.

Her presence still wanders through those meadows;
Her voice still whispers in the breeze,
Speaking to nature lovers' souls
Who read those pages of her diary,
Relive that beauty she so admired.

The Star

Star in heaven, how you shine,
Free from fear in love divine,
Dazzling there in time and space,
Fill souls on earth with glorious grace.

Darkness fades, you disappear,
Then appear as the morning tear
Sparkling on each sunny leaf,
Kindle the spirit's unbelief.

When you shine your shafts of light
Through the church's window bright,
Casting shadow from your cross,
You beat Satan and his lost.

Down the chancel to the nave,
Voices whisper from the grave,
Wrestle with those powers below,
Not able to douse your heavenly glow.

When you hear the organ roar,
Feel it shake the cold stone floor,
All the stained glass glows like fire;
Holy seraphs inspire the choir.

Here you like the people to look
Where eagle's wings bear holy book;
Words of wisdom fill its pages,
Guide those prophets down the ages.

Star in heaven how you shine,
Free from fear in love divine;
Dazzling there in time and space,
Fill souls on earth with glorious grace.

A Childhood Nightmare

One night I dreamed a dream of terror
When floating leaves swept me away
Into the pitch blackness of night;
I screamed aloud for light of day.

I landed inside a patch of marrows
On the ground, in a strange dark soil;
Humidity drenched my lifeless body,
I felt my blood almost boil.

Death reigned in this astral garden;
All I did was lie and brood
Among strange vegetables and fruit,
Not knowing this was demons' food.

Marrows glowed in a demonic pulse,
Drawing energy from planet zones;
This garden glowed in evil charm
That fertilized young children's bones.

I saw a shadow of a horned demon,
His brimstone breath stifled the air,
Felt his teeth sink into my flesh,
Put an end to my bad nightmare.

Dance of Death

I saw the sun's red half
Behind the Devil's Inn;
I walked up this crooked path,

Enjoying this merry din,
When voices pierced the air,
Here in this place of sin.

I saw a violinist there,
A girl danced through a door,
With shining raven hair;

What a beautiful whore!
Her features seemed to glow,
Made my senses soar.

My soul had sunk so low
And soon became beguiled,
There in the music's tempo.

I watched that violinist smile,
Playing that wicked waltz;
The pitch had grown so wild,

It seemed to control my pulse;
My evil feelings woke,
I knew all that was false.

When the darkness spoke,
I found myself obsessed,
And further dread evoked;

For my soul wouldn't rest,
When she gave a shriek,
Danced like one possessed.

I watched her frenzied feet
Dance to music from hell,
I cursed its demonic beat.

I'd fallen under its spell;
It took away my breath
When the darkness fell.

She danced herself to death.

Counterfeit Trinity

Falling stars and blood red moon,
Dragon crouches upon the shore,
Watching the sea's restless womb,
Beast comes out with a mighty roar.

It features the fierceness of a leopard,
Glorifies warlike victories of Greece,
Swooping down upon its prey,
Success comes through this speedy beast.

How it trudges with bear-like feet,
Crushes the weak, builds its empire,
Persia's pride, its satraps of power,
There in the dragon's flames of fire.

Lion's golden mane of Babylon
Reaches the heights of tyranny,
Expresses its stance in idol worship,
Which has become the Vatican's key.

Its seven giant horns of ultimate power,
This last evil emperor of Rome,
Proudly wears his ten kings' crowns;
World becomes his kingdom and throne.

Earth now cracks and it splits asunder,
Out of the abyss, like a battering ram;
All full of rage this false prophet
Roars like a dragon, two horns like a lamb.

He calls fire down from heaven,
Doing many signs and wonders,
Brings worship to the beast's giant statue,
Which moves in flashes of lightning and thunder.

Everybody that receives the mark
From the counterfeit trinity –
Six hundred and sixty-six –
All will blaze in hellfire's fury.

Apocalypse

Darkness fell on the church's spire.
Hark, the clanging icy bell,
Requiem sung by a dissonant choir,
That overshadowed the funeral knell!

The sun went black at eventide,
Burst in giant red ball of flame;
Lightning flashed in the floors of heaven
When stars fell like golden rain.

Grim-faced moon turned blood red,
Demonic horsemen filled the skies,
Galloping like fury through the thunder;
How the power glowed from their eyes!

This chaos touched dear Mother Earth,
Then it quaked and ravaged her womb,
Flattened all the graveyard stones;
Zombies crawled out of her tomb.

Luminous fairies there in the fields,
Once hidden, now are seen,
Flew around with whirring wings
While elves danced on the village green.

Smoke poured out Saint Wilfred's well,
Brimstone from a dragon's breath;
He roared around in the bowels of hell,
There ready to fill the earth with death.

A coven of thirteen wailing witches
Welcomed the spirits on Hangman's Hill,
Rode around on their besom brooms,
Now taken up with the Devil's will.

Children reached the heights of magic,
Despised all innocence and hope,
Saw white for black and black for white,
All wrapped in evil's dark, hooded cloak.

The people huddled together in fear
In the heart of apocalypse,
Watched the false prophet and beast
Appear, deep from the fiery abyss.

Ancient Man

Down on a snowy mountain slope,
The trees all bare and black,
They stood so still in winter's freeze
That made their branches crack.

Through a long and dreary winter,
Ghosts sang their songs of death,
That touched the raging fire below,
Spewed forth like dragon's breath.

High in lonely mountain peaks,
Glacier ghosts all growled;
Farther down in an ancient forest,
Gathering wolves all howled.

An eagle soared through lofty crags
High above the struggling earth,
Groaned and shook in psychic power
That foretold the coming birth.

Way deep down in an icy gorge
Stood ancient newborn man;
How he thrived in nature's power,
He soon took over the land.

Showers of stars fell straight from heaven,
The full moon shone so bright;
Ancient man, who wallowed in wonder,
Now soul power reached its height.

Death of Innocence

A group of children leapfrog all the way
Through the summer flowers in fresh green fields,
Stare at an oak's dead branches, spread like evil
Hands that clutch beneath a cloudless blue sky.
Children in demon masks, who dance and sing,
"Ring a ring o' roses, a pocket full
Of posies, a-tishoo, a-tishoo, we all fall down."

The children gather beneath an old gnarled oak,
Watching crows perched on its bleached branches;
They feel the surge of life in its death-like stillness
That sends its wave of tyranny through the air.
Children delight in its overwhelming power;
They parade with flowers woven in their hair,
Dance beneath a demon's wings of darkness.

Excited children run through the meadows
And go to a midsummer common fair,
Each of them so thrilled by demonic voices
When they take a ride on a merry-go-round,
Watching their faces laugh in flashing lights;
Children wallow in this mystery and fun,
Repeating demons' words, that black is white.

They watch some Druids gather at Stonehenge;
See the sun's red ring in the summer solstice,
Shining there in the centre of standing stones,
Hear ancient voices whisper in the shadows,
Sending ecstasy through their innocent souls,
Reaching those heights in the midsummer sun,
Feel the power of ancient gods from Satan.

The children play chicken on motorways,
Dice with death on this civil engineering,
Then go beneath the bridges, fouled in graffiti,
Read out several names of demonic powers;
Hear their heartbeat back inside the city,
The children go to graves to summon spirits,
That rise beneath their black velvet blanket.

Sleeping City

Demonic horseman rides through the night sky,
Mocking the horned red moon blushing in shame,
Preys on the earth with his eagle eye,
Setting those vaults of high heaven aflame,
Flapping his leathery wings so stealthily,
Gliding over a church's grey tower,
Seeks to terrorise the sleeping city,
Fuelled to the brim with devastating power,
Sniffing wet streets and damp lit roofs,
Landing inside the old city park,
Scorching the earth with his cloven hooves,
Here at one with his beating black heart.
Then he arrives at the cemetery gate,
Dances between those dull leaning graves,
Finding his spirit all burning in hate,
Revelling among the teenagers' raves,
Where he's mingling with popular culture,
Among the twanging electric guitars,
Standing there as bald as a vulture,
Under the dome of the falling stars;
He's so stirred by its rhythmic beat,
And the performer's dark, haunting rap,
How it's inflaming hell fire's red heat;
Spreads out his wings like a giant-sized bat,
Being so wrapped up in satanic sound,
Making the heavens and earth vibrate,
Rattling those skeletons underground,
Summons dead bodies about to wake;
Then he rouses those legions from hell.
He invites them to a midnight fair,
To ride with him on a carousel,
Whizzing around through the evil air,

Mimic screams from ghost train so dire,
Throwing his magical sparks with such zeal,
Laughs at big wheel that is catching on fire
And it spins like a Catherine wheel.
He disappears in a blinding flash,
Rising in smoke to the cloudy heights,
Ready for ultimate kingdom clash,
Thunder booms and the lightning strikes
Over the earth and he shows no pity,
Death now reigns in the sleeping city.

Christian Epics and Poems

This section begins in the age of chivalry at the time of the Order of the Garter, followed by the Teutonic Knights in search of the Holy Grail. The final adventure takes place just after the Napoleonic war, when a clockmaker finds the eternal Spirit.

The collection finishes with some reflective poems, offering love, joy and peace!

The Quest of Sir Robert Marville

Young Robert ran through his county of Shropshire,
Down by the River Severn, past Tinker's Hill,
To see a blacksmith work by his forge fire.
He watched a sword glowing on the anvil,
Fired up his virtue to fight against all evil.
This boy fought with wooden shields and swords,
High in castle towers with the sons of lords.

As a youth he went to Peterhouse in Cambridge,
Adored its gardens, listened to music and poetry;
A keen scholar pursued all kinds of knowledge.
He went hunting with hounds and loved falconry,
Unhorsing many knights at a summer tourney,
Received great honour in the way he served,
Order of the Garter from Edward the Third.

He loved to see his Amy in flowing dresses,
Her twinkling blue eyes just like a bright spring day,
The way her hair hung down in golden tresses;
With cheeks so fresh and pink, as blossom in May,
That angel face as she knelt in chapel to pray.
He met her in the rose garden by chance,
After those gruesome wars he'd fought in France.

Sir Robert had missed his lover for so long,
When she walked so gracefully down the stair,
Grieved to hear those minstrels singing their song
About his beloved's features so fine and fair,
Her movements of such a light and delicate air;
He cursed the wicked Black Prince, the rascal,
That day he snatched her there at Ludlow Castle.

One morning he rode his horse through summer fields,
Clad in armour that glittered in the sunlight,
Three wolf heads were blazon on his shield.
He'd slain many with lance and sword in a fight,
Now faced the greatest challenge of his life;
Found his striving soul just wouldn't rest,
Welcomed many dangers he'd meet in his quest.

He often dreamed about their favourite meadow,
When she came running in her scarlet cloak,
Between the yellow cowslips' bells aglow,
Where she danced beneath the shady oak,
Then fell down laughing on violets' slope.
He thought of this, when riding a winding road,
There under the skies of red and mauve.

When he saw her grace King Edward's court,
Adorned in her draping green satin and silk,
Inspiring many a playful and stirring thought,
Her bosom heaved, soft and white as milk.
His thoughts in that rose garden would never wilt,
Her soul as pure and innocent as a dove,
That filled his heart with a deep and noble love.

At night he heard a hooting tawny owl
Inside a spinney, deep in a moonlit vale,
Disturbed by some wolves, that began to howl,
That seemed to make the full moon shine so pale.
He saw a dragon, bright red from head to tail,
Beating its wings that rustled the grass and leaves,
Smelt its fiery brimstone stifle the breeze.

He gazed at shafts of light that shone from heaven
Through the open windows of heaven's hall
When he rode his horse by the River Severn,
Met an angel standing thirty foot tall;
He realized the time had come to give his all,
Asked to be forgiven for his sin,
Blood of Jesus to make him pure within.

He heard the Holy Spirit's tongues of fire
Moving like a rushing wind in the trembling air,
Touching him, now he'd met the true Messiah,
Glad that God had answered his heartfelt prayer
And given him a living faith to share;
When Jesus melted his dark and sinful heart,
Any sign of evil just had to depart.

Every one of his heavy burdens lifted,
Excelled those happy moments of his youth,
Now drunk in the power of the Holy Spirit,
Glad he'd been girded with the belt of truth.
He'd face any fiends, however uncouth,
For his belt would aid him in his darkest hours,
Well able to fight against demonic powers.

This fired his soul and spurred him on his way;
Later he came to a lively village feast,
Saw some harlequins and jugglers at play,
Laughed when peasants set a gabble of geese
Onto the local sheriff and petrified priest.
He admired those laden stalls of merchandise
And fragrance that came from every type of spice.

When he smelt some brimstone, stood convinced
Unholy fire had blackened this fallow field,
Startled by presence of the Black Prince,
And rampant dragon on his sable shield.
He felt so tempted to order him to yield,
Here in the very heart of his kingdom,
But he'd fight no matter where or when.

Evil spirits paved his way with dread;
He got lost along a narrow track
That came to a dark old castle straight ahead.
He saw some knights inside whose shields were black,
Standing round twelve signs of the zodiac;
He saw a dragon's fire outside a window
That lit up the main hall with an evil glow.

Next morning, he found himself at a tournament
Where evil spirits haunted this unhallowed place;
He faced the dark Black Prince who took off his gauntlet,
Struck him a couple of times around his face,
He felt so angry, his bruised heart quickened in pace,
Overcome with a pending sense of gloom,
And found himself enter this joust of doom.

He heard the silver trumpets' regal sound,
And all the barons, lords and ladies cheered
When his horse's hooves stomped hard on the ground.
He knew it was his enemy the barons revered,
Whom the local crowd of peasants feared.
He found his lance had struck with such a force,
The Black Prince flew backwards off his horse.

He sensed victory was well within his grasp,
Jumped off his horse and swung his mace and chain;
He dealt him deadly blows so thick and fast;
His foe rose to his feet again and again.
He began to think his efforts were in vain
When peasants pelted him with rotten fruit,
Even the lords and ladies followed suit.

A dozen black knights galloped towards him,
But stood his ground and fought with all his might.
He asked the Lord to cleanse his rage within;
His breastplate of righteousness shone so bright
That his enemies were blinded by its light;
Found that God had opened up his way,
Grateful he'd escaped to fight another day.

He came to a Cluniac priory at Much Wenlock,
Chanting monks soon made his spirit soar;
He stood before a door and gave a knock,
Heard a turning key and creaking door,
A monk's lantern lit up the priory floor.
He saw them swing their censers to and fro;
Scenting the air inspired a heavenly glow.

Next morning, he knelt before the altar in prayer;
The bell for sweet prime rang high in the tower,
Singing birds awakened the Shropshire air.
He felt the Holy Spirit come down in power,
Who gave him a vision of Amy in this hour:
Held in a Welsh castle near a forest
By a lake, which filled his heart with zest.

The more he prayed to God, the more he learned
That Jesus Christ had made his faith increase,
Surprised how deep his steadfast spirit burned
Now he'd put on the gospel shoes of peace.
He'd stand there firmly and face any beast,
Whichever paths he'd tread, however odd;
He'd follow right in the footsteps of his God.

He rode under the skies, that were red as hell,
Met a group of folk in ragged cloaks,
Alarmed their leader kept on ringing a bell;
He found this put a damper on his hope.
When their leader hobbled forward and spoke,
He saw the spots on his face that looked so grave,
Almost certain he'd catch this deadly plague.

He thought of scripture, instead of taking flight,
And spoke, "Surely by His stripes I am healed,"
Claimed this disease wouldn't harm this child of light,
Found his strong faith flashing upon his shield,
Blinding the bearers of death, forced them to yield.
He rejoiced to see the beggars driven back,
Their leader turned into a squeaking rat.

After a while he rode through Shrewsbury,
Saw that death knocked hard on every door;
Its people lay around starving and hungry.
He'd never seen so much suffering before,
Here the rules are same for rich and poor;
He passed a pair of millstones that ground in vain,
Now their granite jaws were starved of grain.

He hated Famine, who walked those sombre streets,
Watched him load some corpses onto his wagon;
This awful meeting almost made him weep,
Thought from this evil there is no freedom,
Surely one of the worst sights under heaven;
When man is reduced to a state of living dead,
See his body has been starved from any bread.

Now he's placed again in mortal danger,
That anybody who'd met with Famine must die;
He fought against his gripping pangs of hunger,
Cursed there wasn't any food to buy.
He shrugged his broad shoulders, gave a sigh,
Faced Famine, "Through you, death is rife.
But Jesus said, 'I am the bread of life.'"

He came to a manor a mile from Offa's Dyke,
Dismounted his horse and felt as heavy as lead
When fallen angels swooped from a great height;
These demons of pride filled his heart with dread,
Knowing Satan, the cherubim, was their head.
He had to go inside to pursue his quest
And he went through a door all full of unrest.

When he saw the demons of darkness strike,
Released their power in mighty peals of thunder,
Forks of lightning lit up the Manor that night.
He saw them standing around in suits of armour,
Their blazing eyes almost quenched his valour;
When the powers of the wicked shadowed his hope,
Black pitch burst in flames around the moat.

Somehow he escaped from that evil place,
Saw the sun shine on a garden of flowers,
Now being filled with a full measure of grace,
There risen in Christ's resurrection power.
He drank from fountain of life in this joyful hour,
A sparkling blue lake before him seemed so still,
His spirit anchored to the Father's will.

Later on he came before the tree of life,
Bore the fruit of the Spirit that he'd produced
Through all his deeds of longsuffering and strife,
So glad he'd escaped the evil demons' noose.
He heard a voice come from a white-bearded recluse:
"You're transformed by renewing of your mind;
You're able to fight with beasts of any kind."

There underneath the silver moonbeams
He saw a maiden draped in black satin,
Thought he'd met the lady of his dreams,
Gazing on her bosom, that stirred him within,
But knew this passion would drag him into sin.
He stood before her, started licking his lips,
Found his sensuality so hard to resist.

His heart was beating so fast and his throat ran dry;
He wondered who this charming maiden could be.
He heard her seducing spirit speak, "It is I.
Come enjoy the softness and warmth of my body,
Explore sweet love's pleasure and set yourself free."
But he rebuked his lust in Jesus' name
And saw her body consumed in a sheet of flame.

He met another maiden down the road,
Seemed so bent on bolting and barring his way,
Watching her streams of magic power that flowed,
Heard her say her name was Morgan La Fay,
That Celtic legend should have the final say,
Promised all his victories would be assured –
But he refused her offer of Arthur's sword.

Then he said, "I put no trust in the past,
Shun the faith of any kind of deity.
I've been born into a kingdom that will last
And reject your magic and wicked sorcery;
My helmet of salvation has set my mind free."
He saw her features wrinkled like an old hag's,
Her body collapse into a heap of rags.

Once again he faced the wicked Black Knight
Beneath the Wreakin, this Prince of Shropshire,
Poising as Prince of Darkness and angel of light;
He feared this demon's strength would never tire,
That came straight out from hell's burning fire.
He saw the coat of arms on his sable shield,
But he wondered if he would ever yield.

He rode his horse like fury, pointing his lance,
Struck the wicked Black Prince with such a force,
Then he drew his sword and made his advance
Towards his foe who'd fallen off his horse.
He seized his chance; the battle took its course.
He struck his opponent's sword, and how it rang,
And blows upon his shield made more of a clang.

He dealt the Black Prince such a hefty blow,
Amazed to find he'd fought with such vigour;
He gazed in horror upon his fallen foe
When his black blood oozed out of his armour,
Even some moths flew out of his open visor;
He saw his rotting flesh had turned to dust
And his suit of armour turned red with rust.

This mighty battle he'd fought had made him weak,
He found the Black Prince sprung another surprise,
When he saw him rise again to his feet
And once again he stared in his evil eyes.
He hated to hear this fiend's defiant cries;
He swung his sword of the Spirit with all his might,
Put that wicked beast and his horse to flight.

Later he found himself in a mountain pass,
The Welsh mountains loomed so green and grey,
Here the sense of danger made him gasp,
Saw a falcon swooping onto his prey;
He stopped and knew inside this would be the day.
Yonder he saw a castle beside a lake
And fiendish creature that left its glistening wake.

He saw the dragon tread upon the shore,
Breathing forth a fierce flurry of flames,
That raised his head and gave a deafening roar.
He almost forgot his beloved bound in chains,
When fear rose in his heart and numbed his brain,
But heard her screams and knew this was the hour,
Saw her waving high in the castle tower.

He felt a cold breeze from flapping leathery wings
Flying higher into a black dense cloud,
Amazed to hear so many wicked beings;
How those heavens flashed and quaked so loud!
He watched that dragon bring down his evil crowd,
Soon offer his Lady as a sacrifice,
Glorify the evil of the Antichrist.

He cringed before that army of demonic knights,
Smelt brimstone come from their steaming breath,
Rode there under red skies to the religious rites
That led to this ceremony of eternal death.
Deep down he knew there wasn't much time left,
Crashes of thunder echoed in this raging storm,
There he heard the Devil's battle horn.

When he came to a castle beyond the ridge,
He heard some squeaking chains in the portcullis
As he stepped onto a wooden drawbridge;
The dragon spewed his flames, like fire from the abyss,
But his shield soon quenched those flames with a hiss.
He somehow evaded its evil snapping jaws
But he stood there wounded by its claws.

Then he thought that surely his quest would fail
When he saw the scales on the dragon's back,
Only just missed the fury of his arrow tail,
Wondered what weakness did this creature lack;
He heard him speak before his final attack,
"I'm the Black Prince and have met you thrice,
Now you're burnt and bleeding, where's your Christ?"

Once again he raised his shield of faith,
Summoned his strength, began to move forward;
His armour of God was shining, he felt so safe,
Wielding holy fire from his spiritual sword,
Found this victory was granted from the Lord.
His glowing sword soon pierced the dragon's hide;
Flames were spewing out from his scaly side.

At last he ran up the spiral stone steps in a tower;
There at the top he found and turned a key
To unlock her chains, and broke the demonic power;
Delighted he'd set his distressed damsel free,
He kissed and caressed his overwhelmed lady,
Took her to his horse, hidden along a track,
Rode away so swiftly and didn't look back.

He rode through a sunny vale at Llangollen
To a monastery at the Valley Crucis,
Listened to plainchant sung by Cistercians,
All lost in wonder in this heavenly bliss.
He knelt before the altar and praised Jesus,
Thanked Him for Amy, who became his beloved wife,
Pledged he'd cherish her for the rest of his life.

Our Walk Through Life

We climb a gate, step over a stile,
Into the presence of bees and butterflies,
Walk through those meadows, mile after mile,
Through leafy woods to flowery banks that rise;
Passing a winding stream, sparkling like gems,
Enough to excel a hundred diadems.

Beneath an arch of budding roses, we walk,
Through a garden gate of a stately home,
Stand together among those fragrant flowers,
Where both our characters soon become known,
When the sun highlights the garden's hue,
That lights the splendour and beauty of our virtue.

We love to see the yellow flowering clematis
Climbing over a garden's red brick wall;
We walk so close together, arm in arm,
See a golden shaft of sunlight fall
Along a shady wooded bluebell path,
And hear the youthful voices of spring laugh.

One day we'll be in the Lord's heavenly mansion,
Admiring the symmetry round our gilded room,
Listening to saints and myriad of angels rejoicing,
See each other flourish in perfect bloom;
But will we still remember our love and care,
All those precious moments we used to share?

Those streets we'll walk are paved in glittering gold
Inside the city of the New Jerusalem;
Pass those pearly gates and walls of virtue,
Sparkling with every kind of precious gem;
We'll see those holy angels gathering in a throng,
Hear them singing in perfect plainchant and song.

We'll see the river of life, clear as crystal,
Flowing from the throne of God and Lamb;
Both of our joyful faces will be shining
Among the centuries of saints before the I Am;
Our renewed spirits, souls and bodies will soar,
We'll worship and sing our praises for evermore.

Fiery Angel

Fire flows round an angel's waist;
His muscular body gleams in gold,
The glory of God shines on his face,
And his mighty wings unfold;
His light shining like spokes of a wheel,
When heaven's gates swing open wide,
Then every sensitive soul can feel
Heaven's power as their personal guide.

He lights the path on Pilgrims' Way,
Heightened by God's celestial powers,
Loves to see those lambs at play,
Jump around the flowery meadows.
He flies along to a monastery garden,
That gilds every leaf and hue;
His blessings rise up like a fountain,
Bring sparkle to the morning dew.

He enters through a monastery door
With Holy Spirit's tongues of fire,
Joins in praise that shakes the floor,
Lifts up the chorus of a choir:
"Worthy, the Lamb of God once slain,
Took on sin and death alone,
Jesus who died and rose again,
His angel rolled away the stone."

God's Gift

Infant holy,
Pure and lowly,
Jesus comes from above;
King of all
Lies in a stall,
Shines in Father's love.

God so caring,
Shepherds sharing,
Stand, adore and sing,
Watch these wonders,
Baby slumbers,
Praise the heavenly King.

Star is burning
Wise men learning,
God's most loving gift;
Holy Ghost,
Perfect host,
All the heavens lift.

Secret Place

I love to worship Jesus Christ,
Find his depth of love and grace,
Then think about His sacrifice,
Rest there inside that secret place.

Sometimes I kneel down in prayer,
Where streams of living water flow,
Then feel His presence fill the air
And see the golden seraphs glow.

Right here inside the heart of heaven,
My lifelong faith puts down its roots;
I walk around this beautiful garden
And taste the Holy Spirit's fruits.

Those times I feel so close to Him,
Blessed by His depths of love and grace;
His word now buds so deep within,
Now flowers inside that secret place.

Three Wise Men

Three wise men all follow a star,
Journey for weeks that seems so far,
Their camels tread the desert sand
That brings them into the holy land.

These well-travelled three wise men
Enter those gates of Jerusalem,
Make their way to Herod's feast
And talk about the star in the east.

Soon after they pitch their tents at night
And sleep beneath the desert starlight,
Their Lord God warns them in a dream;
They learn about King Herod's scheme.

Right before the three wise men,
The star rests over Bethlehem.
That shining star points down below;
It lights the stable in heaven's glow.

They gaze upon the infant's face
And enter into the holy place,
Then bow before the King of Kings,
Blessed creator of all things.

They bring their gifts before their Host –
Father, Son and Holy Ghost –
Bring gold, frankincense and myrrh,
Foretell events that will occur.

His Wounds

Our Saviour sweated drops of blood,
He knew His Father's will,
And bore His cross through Zion's streets,
To die on Calvary's hill.

Our Lord was mocked by priests and crowds,
Cruel soldiers scourged His flesh;
Those open wounds that bled for man
Would prove to heal and bless.

When He hung upon that cross,
Nails pierced His hands and feet;
He'd drunk the pain from Father's cup,
That Shepherd for his sheep.

A crown of thorns pressed on His head,
The blood ran down His face;
Our Saviour bled for all mankind,
He gave His love and grace.

His arms outstretched upon the cross
Embraced a world of sin,
He bowed His sacred head in shame,
All that burdened Him.

A Roman soldier thrust his spear
Into our Saviour's side;
And streams of blood and water flowed
From King of Kings who died.

Wedding Supper of the Lamb

Jesus' church now stands complete;
We sit and worship round his feet
At wedding supper of the Lamb,
Before the One who's called 'I Am'.

Beneath the heaven's rainbow light,
We're all arrayed in robes of white;
All praise the Lamb, He conquered sin,
There between the cherubim.

Father sits on His throne of gold;
His blessings spring forth sevenfold.
We stand beside the crystal sea,
Fix our gaze in eternity.

His holy angels pluck their lyres,
Inspire a thousand praising choirs;
We join our hearts in one accord,
Praise Jesus Christ our Lord.

A Prayer

Loving Father, hear our prayer,
Make the church throughout as one;
Serve our brother, sister, preacher,
Shine the light from your dear Son.

Father, Son and Holy Spirit,
Teach us worship, prayer and praise,
Kneeling, bowing down before you,
Die to self in all our ways.

Jesus moves in tribe and nation;
Saviour cleanse us from our sin,
Stir the Lamb and Lion inside us;
Make us holy, pure within.

Make us soar on wings like eagles,
Praise the Lamb before the throne,
See the seraphs ever singing
Here above in heaven's home.

Breathe, oh, breathe the loving Spirit;
Angels sing among our choir;
Heal our land, make people prosper,
Send the holy tongues of fire.

Holy angels, blow the trumpets!
Jesus comes, the clouds will part.
Christian spirits rise in glory,
Heaven's joys fill our hearts.

Resurrection Power

Jesus lay inside a tomb
For three long days and nights,
But from the darkness, death and gloom,
He brought eternal life.

He took on death and sin alone,
His name Immanuel;
His angel rolled away the stone,
He beat the powers of hell.

He walked along Emmaus road,
Now He'd risen from the dead;
The two men's eyes were opened up,
Then He broke the bread.

There on the shore at Galilee,
Jesus prepared a meal;
Peter and John ran through the sea.
It filled their hearts with zeal.

Jesus ascended into heaven
Before his disciples' eyes;
He promised one day He'd return
And fill the earth and skies.

New Jerusalem

See the heavenly Jerusalem
Sparkling with every kind of gem –
Its streets and pavements glittering in gold,
Stately mansions shining so bold
In the kingdom of God and Christ.
Peace and joy reign in this paradise.
The city garden so fresh and green,
Those flowers all glowing in between;
Each colour shines in beauty and truth,
Sparkling fresh with eternal youth.
The tree of life bears its fruits,
Crystal River waters its roots.
Hark, the seraphs sing their chants!
See the Lord Almighty plants
His footsteps deep in the ravine,
Makes the thunderous waterfalls ring,
Hammering the rocks like an anvil
That shakes every mountain and hill.
Rainbows in those waterfalls,
Rising spray that so enthrals;
Listen to its majestic roar,
Makes the holy seraphs soar;
Their harmonies echo in heaven's dome
And melody sparkles in every gem
There in the New Jerusalem.

The Prize

My breastplate bore a sable cross over white,
Shone as I rode beneath those evening skies blood red
With my battle worn army of Teutonic knights;
My heart was weary, my horse's hooves as heavy as lead.
I hated war and wandered around for weeks and weeks,
Wending my way through miles of evergreen forest,
Lush valleys, breathtaking mountains, crags and creeks,
By serpentine rivers that ran over the rocks in zest.
I hadn't seen head nor hide, neither town nor village;
Those many times I wondered whether I'd live or die,
When at last those castle towers appeared on a ridge
And a damsel in the ramparts caught my eye.

That night I feasted inside a lavish banqueting hall,
Drank my tankard of mead and ate some wild boar,
Amused by jesters making shadows on the wall;
How I loved this fun and rest from fortunes of war.
I watched a large log fire crackling, hissing with heat,
Noticed how the mumbling voices all went mute
When the king rose in his regalia onto his feet,
Quick as a flash and my knights and I soon followed suit.
I heard him speak about a quest in Slavonic lands
And not that far away, straight as the crow flies;
I knew how much he wanted the Grail in German hands,
Bring peace and power to his kingdom with this prize.
After I'd tasted the pleasures of the royal rich food,
Sat back and entertained by an Arthurian play,
Where the courtly music heightened my festive mood,
Which helped to raise my spirits, to face another day.

How I loved watching the damsel plucking her harp,
Hearing her soft voice soaring like an eagle's wings,
The way her shining face had
    touched and softened my heart,
She seemed fresh as a shepherdess
    by those bubbling springs.
I admired her golden hair glistening in candlelight,
Her cheeks blushed in a reddish pink
    like the skies at sunrise,
And she danced around in a gown of green and white.
I rose and gazed so fondly into her dark blue eyes,
My passions burned and blazed like a wild forest fire,
Began to curse my vows and my monastic way of life,
My heart and flesh melted and filled me with desire;
I loved this damsel and longed to take her for my wife.

I sank into bed soon after the midnight bell,
Dreamt about my mission, that turned to a nightmare,
Stood on a ferry crossing, a river of fire in hell,
Under demons' wings all beating high in the air,
Saw ghostly Saracens on horseback about to raid
The damned spirits of the departed Teutonic knights
All killed from a battle fought in a past crusade.
I stood on the ferry, horrified by this awesome sight,
Heard their souls scream in a bone dry riverbed,
That echoed between the rocks,
    gripped my soul in torment,
Saw the religious corpses singing mass for the dead;
I wondered if this river of fire would ever relent.

At last I wandered, so weary, over those thirsty plains,
Came to some ashes smouldering like a funeral pyre;
Demonic spirits shackled my hands and feet in chains,
Cracking their whips,
    that drove me towards a lake of fire.
I awoke, aware I'd become a warrior monk through fate,
Thought my monastic life had been to no avail.
My soul became like a dried up well, so desolate;
The only way is to search and to drink from the Grail.

I loved the bite in the autumn air that seemed so crisp,
Hearing my knights all thundering across the drawbridge,
Seeing the countryside enshrouded in morning mist;
The sun's red wheel peeped high over a mountain ridge.
After an hour I came to a ritual burial mound,
Enhanced by silver birches, among some scented pine;
When the grey mists faded, tension mounted all around,
Now magic runes glowed on the rocks in a Saxon shrine.
My horse sweated, snorted and reared
    at a presence of evil;
I met with Woden's ghost in his broad-brimmed hat.
My ancestral Saxon spirit rose and conquered my will,
When the light began to fade and those skies went black.
Thor's mighty hammer flashed, so high in the welkin,
Lit some Slavonic knights I saw upon the plain,
Heard my knights galloping along in such a din.
I raised my sword against the Slavs to kill or maim,
Until sparks flew off their helmets and steel breastplates;
I slew so many it seemed as though the earth had bled,
Evil pride and zeal had brought my soul to hate,
And death brought ravens and red kite soaring overhead.

Through most of that week,
   my spirit was filled with remorse.
Still thinking about the battle, blood and aftermath,
I came across a man riding his dappled horse,
Followed him through the bogs onto a perilous path;
My soul was dark and distressed at the low-lying fog,
Even more alarmed to see my guide disappear.
I saw some ogres hissing in a bubbling bog;
Slimy water dripped down their matted beards,
Looked as though something had
   pecked and pitted their flesh.
Above I saw some ravens in branches of a gnarled oak
Squawk at a woman in black
   who spoke like a prophetess,
Pointing her skeleton finger from the sleeve of her cloak
At the mistletoe's leaves – and there I saw the Grail
Shining in splendour; it dazzled me with its golden light.
It touched my heart and turned my face so ghastly pale;
I stood in wonder gazing upon this awesome sight,
Stunned by the waters turning to a bright green mist
Underneath the red and purple evening skies,
Among the marshes' blue lanterns from will-o'-the-wisp,
Shocked by the rising living dead with bloodshot eyes;
Made those black bogs spit, like a witch's cauldron.
I saw some knights reach for the Grail
   and sink to their death;
Told the rest of my men to flee this evil deception,
And those ogres chased my men with steaming breath.

I cursed the freezing weather in the mountains that night,
Where demons whined in a bitter wind
    that wrinkled the snow;
The moon came out and created pictures
    in black-and-white
That shone upon the monastery down in a valley below.
I watched those ravens peck at food outside the kitchen,
Heard the bell for vespers and plainchant being sung,
Pleased I'd found some food and shelter for my men.
I banged upon the door above where icicles hung;
An abbot's lantern led me to a Saxon shrine,
Where spring water flowed
    from the vault of Saint Redwold;
His spirit shone in a golden shaft of light divine,
But his phials of blood, hair and nails had left me cold.
I watched some candles flickering in the saint's presence,
A group of monks all chanting on this Candlemas night,
Led by a couple of brothers,
    swinging their smoking censers;
Raised their drooping hoods
    and their faces went all white,
Like skulls of death, with round eyes glowing in dark red.
I heard the liturgy spoken in Latin – it sounded so holy –
The priest ringing a Sanctus bell to wake the dead.
I ate the sacred emblems before the Lord Almighty,
Thought about them turning back to His flesh and blood;
Upset at Him being sacrificed all over again.
These superstitions were dark
    and made my heartbeat thud;
Surely He rose from the dead and took away our blame.

Moonlight shone in my small cell window onto the floor;
I felt a nagging presence of an unwelcome guest,
Saw that Saxon Saint standing at my door
Holding a leather whip in his hand, and flayed my flesh.
I winced in pain again and again
    from those stinging cords,
Refused to accept this penance for my state of unbelief,
Found myself soon calling on the Lord of Lords,
Who forgave my sin, came in my heart and took my grief.
The saint went in a flash; my spirit was set aflame,
To think the light of the world stood
    at the foot of my bed,
And when the power of the Holy Spirit finally came,
He breathed his hallowed tongues of fire upon my head.

Early morning, I gazed at the rugged mountaintops,
Frozen in majesty beneath the sunny skies so blue,
Thrilled at those raging rivers roaring between the rocks.
I met some shepherds in fresh green valleys
    sparkling with dew,
Watched their fingers move up and down
    on their wooden pipes,
Playing songs of the earth with mirth
    in this season of spring,
Brought the forces of nature in my soul to sheer delight,
And maidens danced around a maypole in a ring.
I went ahead and came to an overhanging crag,
Saw Hearne the hunter's antlers among six sacred oaks,
The Green Man's burning torch
    that made the ravens nag
Above some bearded Druids in white, hooded cloaks;
Performed a sacrifice on an altar encircled with stones.

I heard a scream pierce those corridors of time
And nature's evil gods soon made their presence known.
I stood where Beltane's smouldering ashes
   were left behind.
The skies went dark; I gazed into the vaults of heaven;
There was a terrific roar and I saw a furnace of flames,
A hundred fast-approaching demons' skeleton horses
Snorted flames of fire as the riders lashed their reins;
I flinched when this huge macabre army filled the skies.
They fell upon my knights,
   wielding their weapons of war;
They scared me out of my wits with their evil battle cries.
I slew so many of them but they still came back for more;
Even their fatal wounds soon healed
   and they rose to their feet,
Those wicked satanic spirits who'd risen from the dead.
I fought all night, so sapped of strength and faced defeat;
They left soon after the morning sun arose from its bed.

It seemed I rode for days upon a crooked road.
Down in a misty valley, I saw a sleeping town;
My burdens lifted and here I lightened my heavy load.
Beyond I saw a wood and castle on higher ground.
A hermit warned me not to go into this town of sin;
I learned that death was seen on every person's face,
And legions of evil spirits fouled the air within –
Moditch the evil warlock controlled that wicked place.
I learned that inside the castle chapel stands the Grail,
Where thick black steaming pitch
   bubbled round the moat;
Their walls were much too well defended for me to assail,
And if I ordered an attack, I'd stand little hope.

I learned of a pageant that finishes inside the castle wall;
Four of my men and I dressed up in peasants' clothes,
Searched around those streets in town at nightfall
And found some jokers' costumes that cheered my woes.
I hid some swords and shields inside a wooden cart,
Throughout a moonlit night aware of watching eyes,
Almost felt the beating from Moditch's cruel black heart.
Next morning my men and I
    joined the pageant in disguise,
Saw a full sun beaming upon a motley crowd
Of harlequins, and put a smile on every clown.
I rejoiced to see some happy children shouting so loud
At the merry minstrels' music that roused the town,
Found I was able to view the castle walls inside.
I felt uneasy and slipped quickly out of sight,
Relieved I'd found a place in an old wine cellar to hide.
Later I crept up the worn stone steps at midnight;
Golden light shone through cracks in an old oak door;
Once inside the chapel, my eyes were almost blinded,
I fell on my face in awe and how my soul did soar,
Until I saw a pair of horns on a demon's head,
That proved to be a master in the art of disguise.
I thanked my God I was able to discern
    this demonic spirit,
But my men hadn't fathomed out its light and lies;
I grabbed the Grail, that demon laughed himself in a fit
When the sound of guards came rushing up the steps.
I wielded my sword; they fell with such a mighty thud,
Then my heart almost plunged in those shady depths,
Found I almost slipped on the steps, dripping with blood.

My men followed me across the courtyard
   quick as they could,
Went across the drawbridge only just in time;
I was relieved my army had left the shelter of the wood,
All ready at the drawbridge and formed a battle line.

Somehow I kept their soldiers at bay on the drawbridge,
Their numbers began pressing so hard
   I was forced to retire,
Threw a blazing torch in the moat,
   which ignited the pitch,
That burst into black, belching smoke and flames of fire.
I saw their soldiers retreat, the drawbridge was raised;
Alarmed that Moditch waved his wand in a castle tower,
Evoking demons from the depths of hell that blazed
Throughout their fiery plains and caves in sheer power.
I gazed in the vaults of heaven, glowing in brilliant red;
Demon knights came charging with lances pointed ready.
My body shook at seeing those spirits of the dead.
People stood on the castle walls, all cheering this tourney.
I crashed into the demon knights with terrific force;
My men's lances found their mark,
   but splintered or broken.
My foes surprised by our courage and being unhorsed,
I drew my sword out of my scabbard and went for them;
Sensed Moditch had joined forces with princes of the air,
Tormented me with magic, straight from the astral plain.
I despaired and went straight down
   upon my knees in prayer.
I also prayed for my men, who'd begun to feel the strain,

When their knights went berserk
    and much of our blood was shed.
I fretted and feared we'd fallen to such a wicked foe,
For most of my men were wounded or lay around dead.
I saw the powers of darkness fade in a heavenly glow
When some cherubim appeared along with the Messiah,
Riding in chariots of fire, sparkling like precious stones;
Above I saw the glory of God burning like fire,
His crystal sea and a rainbow circled a sapphire throne.
I stood in awe when cherubim struck
    with glowing swords
And freed my knights from
    all those evil powers of darkness.
My men were healed and I gave glory to the Lord;
Answered my prayer, rescued
    and filled my heart with zest.

I rode with my knights through cheering towns,
    hailed as a hero
By our King, rejoiced the Grail was in German hands;
I watched him captured by its power and constant glow,
Regretted he ordered me to conquer those Slavonic lands.
I was crushed at Tannenberg
    and left the Teutonic knights,
Met my damsel down by streams of living water.
I never forgot when she played her harp
    that autumn night,
Found myself betrothed to a nobleman's daughter.

We embraced each other
   under the bright blue dome of heaven,
My wife in her emerald gown,
   and I stroked her golden hair,
Beneath the blue clematis in a walled rose garden,
Smelt those blushing roses scenting the summer air.
We opened a garden gate and went in the countryside,
Greeted there by a high-pitched whistling nightingale;
Walking along with Holy Spirit as our guide,
We gazed upon this beauty so deep within the vale,
And God gave us a vision of the New Jerusalem.
We felt the Father's presence walking among the trees,
The river's music flowed like that in the Garden of Eden;
We stared in wonder at those trees
   and hedges' gilded leaves,
Felt like Adam and Eve in Eden before the Fall,
Saw the whole of creation blossom through Father's eyes
Because our Lord had died outside that city wall;
Now lives so deep within our spirits, and that's the prize.

The First Woe

He watched those cherubim burning in golden light
In their chariots of fire in eternity,
But he fell from heaven like a star that night,

When the Almighty gave him a shining key
To open the shaft of the abyss, that gave a roar,
When the forces of darkness were all set free

From the raging abyss, which made his spirit soar,
When clouds of smoke rose from that fiery furnace
That loosed its rage and fury for evermore.

Black smoke darkened the sky and the sun's red face,
Those locusts bent on battle looked like horses;
Five months they'd torment the human race.

He saw their armies ride out the mouth of the abyss
With golden crowns set upon their evil heads,
Breathe out their fiery brimstone with a hiss.

He followed their horses under those skies of red,
All bearing their lion's teeth and breastplates of iron;
He heard their leathery wings thundering in dread.

Those riders' tails kept stinging like a scorpion,
He served King of the Abyss, angel Apollyon.

Two Hundred Million Horsemen

Four dark angels were unbound
Down at the Euphrates riverbed;
All screamed on unhallowed ground,
Arose in power and shook the dead.
These angels stood in the breaking dawn
When they heard their prophet speak,
Upset the peace before the storm,
Before the coming thunderous hoof-beats
Of two hundred million horsemen,
Breathing plagues and fiery breath.
Those two hundred million horsemen
Rode in the valley, in the shadow of death,
Reaped havoc and wallowing in hate –
That force that drove the Turkish Empire.
They wore red, blue and gold breastplates,
Rode lion-head horses snorting fire,
Smote millions with their snake-like tails
That left a trail of death behind.
In cities, towns, hills and plains,
They'd struck down a third of mankind.

In Search of the Spirit

David opened his hundred-year-old workshop,
All his ticking clocks were chiming nine;
Set about repairing his prized French clock.

Images of war soon flooded into his mind,
Those days he fought in the Napoleonic War.
It seemed to make him relive those moments in time.

Still bothered by those aches and pains he'd borne;
His medal for valour made him a proud man,
His heroism tended to make his spirit soar,

When he advanced in ranks to fight for England,
All in step with thousands of marching feet,
And goose-pimples rose on the back of his hand

From those kettledrums when rolling their beat,
Overwhelming sound of the Scottish bagpipes,
Made his sense of glory seem complete.

When cannons fired from the centre, left and right,
He stood and joined in the volley of musket fire,
And those flashes and flares had blurred his sight.

Somehow that stench of death soon quenched his desire
On the bloody battlefield, below a ridge,
That kept on smouldering like a funeral pyre.

This caused him to set his heart on pilgrimage,
To search for life inside his inner spirit;
Early that morning he left his Cumbrian village.

This pilgrim placed a bible inside his kit,
Walked down a road in his sparrow-tailed coat,
Regretted he'd missed that Oxford scholarship;

But this journey soon filled his heart with hope,
When he smelt that fragrant springtime air,
Thought where Lucy once ran down a slope

With sunlight sparkling on her golden hair,
Seeing her move in her long green summer dress;
Wondered why he'd lost a maiden so fair.

The way her heaving breast prompted his flesh,
He felt the depths of his passion, burning in lust,
All that afternoon he spent in distress.

He found his hopes and dreams had crumpled to dust,
That night spent in the wicked wayside inn,
Felt so guilty he'd broken the Almighty's trust.

How the lamp of his spirit burned so dim;
Dreamt he came to a Celtic bubbling spring,
Found that pantheism all welled up within.

At Castlerigg he saw a red kite hovering
Above his Lucy, wearing a Celtic gown,
Standing and kneeling before a British king;

Worried to see her wearing a garland crown.
Druid priests also appeared in his dream,
Watched by a Celtic tribe all gathered round.

He saw her placed in a wicker woven in green,
Hanging down an overhanging crag,
That started swinging over a surging stream.

Above he heard some wheeling ravens nag,
Made him sense that Celtic season of Beltane,
When he heard those Druids' tongues all wag.

He watched the wicker basket burst in flame;
Her piercing screams soon forced him to his knees.
He heard her call her Celtic god by name,

Met the Green Man in his garment of leaves.
His burning torch lit up valley and mountain;
He followed him through the thick dark forest trees,

Surprised he'd drifted into a fairy glen,
Where mottled green rocks glistened inside a rill;
Wondered why he'd entered this elfin kingdom.

Elves' toadstools sloped up Greenwood Hill;
He saw their queen gorging her food in the glade,
Then fell asleep after having her fill.

He heard some fairies' music being played,
That whirred above the snoozing elfin king,
Bared his belly in the afternoon shade.

How he admired the fairies on the wing
That brightened those flowers,
    enhanced the summer views;
He stopped, drank from a fresh bubbling spring.

He saw some elves in winkle picker shoes,
Wearing pointed hats, with long white beards,
And danced around a fairy ring in twos.

Early next morning he woke up feeling weird,
When he saw the elfin king's spirit
Flash and crack before he disappeared.

He could still hear the fairies' enchanting music,
Became wearied by its haunting sound;
After breakfast he made his way to Keswick.

He went in the centre of this market town,
Came to an open air stage and saw the mayor
Read a prologue before a gathering crowd.

A curtain opened; he watched some strolling players
Performing a naughty play on some folklore,
Met by a couple of aging soothsayers;

He followed them and his doubts began to gnaw
When he came to a waiting shiny black coach,
Saw an aristocratic crest on its door.

Once inside, he chatted with his host,
Listened to the horses' galloping hooves;
Then he saw the outline of a ghost,

Several demons danced on moonlit roofs,
And those visions sent him over the top.
Next he faced a couple of smiling spooks.

The coach and horses came to a sudden stop.
He found himself inside a castle courtyard,
Saw a weathervane above a castle clock.

Some howling hounds soon put him on his guard,
But taken aback when he faced a mastiff bitch,
Approached him slowly, her eyes all glazing hard.

His nerves almost reached their highest pitch.
Lord Byron answered his knock on the door;
He stood there face to face in world of the rich.

Mozart's music made his spirit soar,
Aristocrats were at this masked ball,
Danced on a black-and-white chequered floor,

Elegance overwhelmed him in this grand hall
Lit by a thousand sparkling chandeliers,
Reflected evil shadows on the wall.

Guests removed their masks and heightened his fears,
Shocked to see the evil light up their eyes,
Cringed when dazzling demons made him all ears;

The world, flesh and the Devil had shed its disguise;
He found their words had filled his heart with dread,
Wondering how long he'd evade their awful lies.

He was given a candle to light his way to bed,
Lay between the sheets and felt alone;
Visions of ancient Britain ran through his head:

Long ago when this land was conquered by Rome,
When pagan rites inflamed the Celtic race,
Those Romano-Celtic gods all set in stone.

All his thoughts that followed he could hardly face,
About those end times in the temple of Jerusalem,
That time the Antichrist sits in that holy place.

He wrote everything down with his feather pen
Just before this evil had reached its height;
Decided to leave the castle there and then,

And ran beneath a pitch black sky that night,
Fiddling round in his pocket for a key,
Knew it would help to shed some further light.

When he came across a haunting sea,
Met a ferryman on the black sand,
Who ferried him to an ancient monastery.

At last he landed somewhere on a hermit's island,
Wandered through a damp and misty moor,
But couldn't see farther than his outstretched hand.

After he climbed some steps, he unlocked a door,
Held his breath and wondered what he'd find;
A ghostly monk shook him right to the core.

There inside he felt a weight press upon his mind,
Came to a library on biblical scholarship,
Read their heresies to deceive mankind.

He stared between some silver candlesticks
At ghostly monks writing with feather pens,
Mumbling Latin words from their trembling lips,

Stood and watched them indulge in doctrines of demons,
Standing in front of their lecterns, in ball and chain.
He despised their bondage to philosophy and reason,

All this learning hammered inside his brain;
He found his self being inflated with pride,
All his previous knowledge seemed in vain.

This newfound sense of power he couldn't hide,
Until he heard the clanging compline bell
That woke him out of his trance-like state inside.

He fell under the religious spirits' spell,
Joined some monks who walked in reverence;
He copied their ascetic traits that came from hell,

Smelt the overpowering burning incense,
Plainchant sung so dissonant and out of time,
Then sensed an all prevailing evil presence

Inside the chapel he came before an evil shrine
Where all the singing monks fell down in awe
Before an idol that seemed and looked divine.

He fled this idolatry straight through a door.
Frosty air soon pierced his face like a draught;
A blanket of fog spread right across a moor

Where he heard some gathering spirits laugh,
And their eyes were shining ever so bright,
Watching him tread a never-ending path.

He walked along this path so full of fright,
Realised how much he'd fallen into sin,
But lights in the distance proved a welcome sight.

Across a harbour he came to the Cutlass Inn,
Loved the way those drunken sailors sang,
And he danced to the hornpipe's merry din.

Then he found himself being press-ganged
And soon bundled on board a whaling ship,
Relieved he'd saved himself from being hanged.

He sailed on surging seas – how he hated this trip,
Down on his knees, scrubbing a blood stained deck,
His broken will still weighing on his spirit.

How long those days dragged on! He felt a wreck,
With blistered hands, dry skin and salt in his nose,
Found he sank in trouble right up to his neck

When thoughts of the cracking leather whip arose,
That time he received twenty lashes twice,
And traces of blood and sweat still stained his clothes.

Later in the week he came to a kingdom of ice,
Floating in a calm sea, sparkling in emerald green;
He revelled in this place of paradise,

All heightened by the noon sun's golden beams,
And those palaces, sparkling glacier blue,
Proved the most majestic sight he'd ever seen.

He felt a changing mood in the restless crew
When the ship rode neither wind nor wave
Before an ancient sun's dark reddening hue,

When he drifted inside an icy cave,
Saw some Vikings frozen in a clear glass wall,
Alarmed to hear their ancestral spirits rave

And Norse language echoed through the hall.
The hubbub grew to such a pitch until
He found he couldn't get to grips with it all.

He welcomed that white wilderness, so still,
When his struggling ship became stuck fast,
Became frozen, set like his stubborn will.

He sought some shelter from an icy blast,
Huddled in his cabin all full of fright,
Wondering how much longer this storm would last,

When he gazed in that world of black-and-white
Under a clear night sky, and thought of escape,
To make his way beneath those northern lights.

He found some snowshoes that gave him his break,
Trudged slowly through the moonlit snow,
Found he'd entered into a world of fate,

When those piercing winds began to blow;
He shook with fear when he saw a polar bear,
Soon made him sick and sink to an all-time low;

Heard white wolves howl in the frosty air,
Came to realise he was running out of time,
Fell down on his knees in deep despair.

He saw a tall ship's mast all covered in rime;
Came to an old rope ladder and climbed on board,
So pleased he'd left his troubled past behind,

Glad the way that cruel ice cracked and thawed.
He felt the timbers creak and the ship in motion,
Revelling in his freedom until his spirit soared,

On this battleship in the Arctic Ocean;
Watched the wind breathe hard in the bulging sails
As he rode the waves that lifted his emotion.

The high seas grew so rough, he grabbed the rails,
Heard a sailor shouting in the crow's nest,
Pointed to a sea serpent whipping its tail;

He saw its sudden strike in the howling tempest
And heard a broadside boom from thirty cannons
That scored a direct hit on the uninvited guest.

It shrieked and sank in pain to fifty fathoms;
Waters writhed and washed over the deck.
He saw blood on the waters, this strangest of omens.

Now filled with fear, he wondered what to expect
When, driven without mercy in a rocky bay,
The ship broke up and became a total wreck.

Driftwood saved his life from the seas that day;
He came across a Saxon ship of the dead
That calmed the seas and moved through mists of grey.

He dragged his body, which felt as heavy as lead,
Inside the ship and thought he was going to die,
Then heard some horses' hooves right overhead,

Saw Woden riding Sleipnir in a clear blue sky,
Followed by screaming Valkyries back from war,
Enter Valhalla's iron gates mounted so high.

A sense of grandeur filled his spirit with awe
When he saw the castle shine bright as the sun
After he stepped off the ship onto the shore.

This powerful stronghold he had to overcome;
First he must regain his strength and wait
His time before this final battle began.

Below this castle he came to a fiery lake,
Went through a forest and passed an old wolves' den
And found some steps that led to a spiked iron gate.

He'd entered Valhalla through a lower region,
And found some food and water outside a cell,
Ate and drank, moved farther through the dungeon,

Almost fell in a bottomless giant-sized well.
He felt the anger in the brimstone air
That fuelled Valhalla's violent fires from hell.

Several ghostly Saxons caught him unawares;
The long dead heroes' faces preyed on his mind.
Being chased up some grey stone spiral stairs,

He found a window, went straight down a vine,
Ran in a wood straight through a rippling stream,
With Woden's bloodhounds howling close behind.

It seemed he was having some terrible dream,
Trying to overcome as he did before;
Came to a chapel covered over in green.

He entered through a creaking old oak door
Touched by sparkling golden hanging cobwebs;
Felt the Almighty's presence like never before.

Once inside the holy sanctuary, and Spirit-led,
He saw a thirty-foot cherubim's wings unfold
And sparkling light streaming from the Godhead.

Before this divine presence of gleaming gold,
He loved the beauty on each cherubim's face,
Saw those redeemed saints and prophets of old.

His spirit praised God for this measure of grace,
Then saw the ready prepared New Jerusalem;
Amazed at the tabernacle set in place,

Overwhelmed by praise in the kingdom of heaven,
Inside his spirit, yet able to gaze without
Into Satan's old world, like a dark chasm,

And saw the wars, what brought them all about,
The plight of fallen angels and depraved man;
All these perceptions left no room for doubt.

Past, present and future had no time span.
He saw the heroes and gods of nations stirred,
Now seemed futile before God's perfect plan.

He saw those visions from God's inspired word,
Ultimate reality here, all in picture form,
Everything so clear and nothing blurred.

He waited for a new heaven and earth to dawn,
When demonic forces will no longer prevail
But burn in the lake of fire's unending storm.

After his vision he saw a ship's white sails,
Went straight to the harbour and boarded a ship;
Later he weighed anchor somewhere in Wales.

A waiting coach took him to the Lake District,
Where mountaintops reflected in the sunlit lake,
Seen from his fresh teaching inside his spirit.

Bright green valleys enhanced his childlike faith,
Like the golden eagle's wings that soared.
When he came to his village at Bassenthwaite,
He met his Lucy waiting by his door.

Now

A nightingale whistles on a bough,
At last I have this moment now,
Rough winds no longer rage from the north,
New white blossom's bursting forth.
Sunlight gentle as a burning lamp,
I'm no weather-beaten tramp,
Wandering along that stony path,
When that waning moon used to laugh,
Now fresh flowers are peeping through,
Sparkle in early morning dew.
Young lambs jumping in springtime air,
Under the mighty Shepherd's care,
Now all those former things have passed;
My Lord Jesus, you have me at last.